D1809149

Mental
Struggles
and
Biblical
Truths

Keri Payne

WESTBOW
PRESS®
A DIVISION OF THOMAS NELSON
& ZONDERVAN

Copyright © 2020 Keri Payne.

All rights reserved. No part of this book may be used or reproduced by any means, graphic, electronic, or mechanical, including photocopying, recording, taping or by any information storage retrieval system without the written permission of the author except in the case of brief quotations embodied in critical articles and reviews.

WestBow Press books may be ordered through booksellers or by contacting:

WestBow Press
A Division of Thomas Nelson & Zondervan
1663 Liberty Drive
Bloomington, IN 47403
www.westbowpress.com
1 (866) 928-1240

Because of the dynamic nature of the Internet, any web addresses or links contained in this book may have changed since publication and may no longer be valid. The views expressed in this work are solely those of the author and do not necessarily reflect the views of the publisher, and the publisher hereby disclaims any responsibility for them.

Any people depicted in stock imagery provided by Getty Images are models, and such images are being used for illustrative purposes only.
Certain stock imagery © Getty Images.

Scripture taken from the King James Version of the Bible.

ISBN: 978-1-9736-9619-3 (sc)
ISBN: 978-1-9736-9618-6 (hc)
ISBN: 978-1-9736-9620-9 (e)

Library of Congress Control Number: 2020912505

Print information available on the last page.

WestBow Press rev. date: 08/10/2020

Dedication

I dedicate this book to my husband Richard for your unconditional love. We never knew what our lives would hold after we said I do. What I do know was that mental health issues would not have been something I thought we would have to deal with. Not only did you make a vow to me on our wedding day but you have lived that vow every day for the past 22 years. In sickness and in health. The sacrifices you have made for me and your willingness to make changes in our lives to help me live the best life I can with my struggles has shown me a love I never knew could exist. God gave me you and I thank him for you every day. You are truly my knight in shining armor and I am blessed to be your wife. All my love, Keri

I also dedicate this book to my amazing boys, Todd and Clay. Every day we wake up is a new day with new struggles and you are always there with a smile. Your understanding and willingness to support me on my darkest days as well as my good ones have left me wondering how I could deserve such two amazing boys. Because of you I have purpose and a drive to always try. Try to get through the day, try to heal, try to be my best self. On the days I fail you are still there always checking to see if I'm okay, listening with encouraging words, a smile and an adventure to bring me out of my darkest place. You two are my greatest accomplishments and I pray you always know how much I love you and how much you mean to me. Love, Mom

Lastly, I dedicate this book to my sister in law Cynthia. You are the first person I came to when the walls came crashing down around me and I didn't know what was happening to me. You were not only there to help me find the answers, but your non-judgmental approach was exactly what I needed to feel safe and not alone. I could have not gotten through this without you and I want you to know how much I value you. You have shown me that there are people out there that do care and are willing to help without judgement and I am so blessed to have you in my life. I love and appreciate you and thank you for all that you do for our family! Love, Keri

Contents

Preface

As I sit in my kitchen looking out the window, I can hear the birds chirping. The sun is shining. The neighborhood kiddos are coming down the driveway on their ATVs to visit, and Julie, the dog, is barking the alarm that someone is here. A smile comes to my face and I thank God for another day to be alive. Then I think back to an earlier time when I was sitting in this same spot. A smile was so out of reach and thankfulness was a state of mind I could not comprehend.

It was so quiet in the house you could hear a pin drop. The sun had already gone down for the day. My husband and sister in law sat in the other room with their heads bowed listening as I answered questions to the man sitting next to me. My body shook uncontrollably. No matter how deep a breath I took, no matter if I paced the floor or rubbed my arms and legs, I couldn't get it to stop. My hands and lips tingled and burned. As well as a spot in the front right side of my brain that felt like someone had lit a fire that could not be put out. Little did I know at that time it was the flow of adrenaline running through my body at such an alarming rate, my blood flow could not keep it concentrated enough. My fight or flight response was in high gear and stuck in "on" mode. I could not shut it off, nor had I the ability to do so. All I wanted it to do was stop. The sleep that evaded me for weeks would not come. The nightmares that woke me every 10 minutes when I tried to close my eyes to get some kind of relief left me terrified and living in a time that I did not want to remember and didn't understand why? Why now? I should feel safe! I should feel good! I should not be out of control! I felt hopeless. This will never end. I can't eat, I can't sleep, I can't have peace no matter what I try. I tried everything the doctors told me to. I've tried dozens of medications, group therapy, sleep schedule, out-patient, test and more tests, cleaning house, exercise, staying busy, detox, surgeries. I even received a nice handout about somatic pain syndrome from my current head doctor and his last words he said to me were, "you need to give yourself time, and believe in the grace you say you do, and I will be gone until next week, so if you need anything we will talk about it then." It was too late. I was too far gone down in *that* darkness and the only thing I had to hold onto was this little light deep down inside that kept saying, "hold on, there is a safe way out of this." I wanted to survive this. I did not want to give up and let this control me. My biggest fear? My pain and suffering were so bad that I may lose what little shred of insanity I had and do something I didn't want to do. Most of all I was afraid I would do something and not realize it, because my mind was begging for relief. I needed something to just ease this pain permanently because I have no help, no answers, no relief, no control. I am completely and utterly alone. Yes, I believe in God, and yes, I have called out to him. I have cried, I have begged and pleaded with Him. I work in the church, I live a Christian life, I don't drink, I don't do drugs, I have prayed for forgiveness every day. I try to love everyone, be what everyone needs me to be. Hold my head up and hide my pain like a good little girl does, but still I wasn't safe. What I truly needed was a safe place. I never would have thought my own home would not be safe, but the fact was it wasn't about the building I was in or the people that lived in it with me. It was about the hollow shell of a body where my mind resided that wasn't safe. All the trauma my body had endured had left me empty: the sexual abuse as a child, childhood bullying, teenage pregnancy, illness after illness, the surgeries, the countless doctor appointments with professionals that had no answers and treated me as if it was all in my head. The never feeling safe and just wanting a safe place to land all left me feeling as though I had to be on alert for the next thing coming. It is what I have always done. The problem was I had nothing left in me to give. I needed a safe place to get some semblance of rest for my body, but my body was not safe from what my mind may drive me to do. The hardest realization was why? I read my Bible every day. I prayed and asked God to take this from me, I prayed for answers for why my body had so much illness in my 38 years. I prayed for relief from my physical pain. I prayed for peace. I prayed for help. And I waited. I vowed I would never give up hope that God would bring me through this. How? I did not know and I was scared. I asked my pastor and all he could say was, "God has a reason and He will see you through this, you just got to trust Him". I know that, but how do I process while I wait? In the midst of this horrible struggle how do I cope? The answers I got were: you should trust, you should not question, you should be content, you should wait, you should have enough faith.

The man across the table from me tilted his head downward, looking at me from over his reading glasses, there was no judgement in his eyes as he asked the question. "Have you made plans on how you may end your life?" Another shudder went through me as I knew my family was listening and there was an overwhelming reality of shame I felt about it. Do I tell the truth to get help? Or, do I hide the answer to protect them. I don't want them to think that they are not enough, but I am suffering so much. The gaze from across the reading glasses held firm in place as he waited patiently for my answer. Dead silence lingered for what seemed like an eternity. Then as quietly as I dared a whisper of yes escaped my lips, but it wasn't low enough for my family not to hear. I heard a heavy sigh from the other room and an even stronger wave of panic overtook me. The disappointment they must have for me, the failure that I have become. Another wave of fear. It won't stop.

After several more questions, He said it was time to go. For a split second I felt something akin to relief, but I hadn't felt that feeling in so long I wasn't for sure if that is what is was. We loaded up and headed to the hospital emergency room where I would start the process to be admitted. Not for a physical cut, or another surgery, but for 24/7 surveillance I needed to guarantee my life would not end on my terms, but on Gods. Supervision not just to protect me, but classes and therapy, and the support I so needed while I waited on the Lord to heed my desperate plea. Two more days came of no sleep, two more days of endless shaking, and two more hospitals later I finally got to the end of the road. This is it. This is where I will heal and wait on God. This is where my healing journey begins. But I still carried a burden with me I knew I had to leave at the door. Judgement. Judgement from others, judgement from myself, and judgement from God. I had to stop dwelling on the judgement and hold to the promise that no matter what, God would love me still. As I enter the doors to the behavioral health unit and began my check-in routine, I had to let go of everything I knew about religion and hold close to the one thing I did know. Jesus loved me! No matter what he loved me and nothing else in my life mattered except that.

In the two weeks that followed I spent all day in group therapy learning what was going on in my body and why I was struggling. It wasn't all the answers I needed, but it was a great start. I got the medicine my body so needed but was denied by the doctor who gave me the somatic pain handout and said my faith was lacking and grace was withheld. I learned that I suffered from a medical condition brought on my genetics, life circumstance and body chemistry. Major depression disorder, panic disorder and complex post-traumatic stress disorder are their names. I learned skills called CBT, DBT, mindfulness, and non-judgmental and started to see improvements. I laid down all those coping skills I used to survive as a child and had held onto for so long and started to replace them with these new skills I was learning, but something was still nagging at my mind. Is this what God wants me to be doing? Are these skills He would approve of? How do these skills measure up in his eyes? Some of these skills are from other religions and I hesitated and withheld myself from practicing them in fear of some crazy conversion would take place and separate me from the love God had for me. I knew something had to change if I was going to survive this.

The first thing to change was my perspective. Perspective on my circumstance and what brought me to this point in my life. The perspective that sometimes you have to let go of what you thought things were and find truth is what you know it is. Truth! How do I find out the truth? The truth on how God sees me and sees my mental health illness and how to move forward with this infirmity I bear. Was this infirmity a true reflection of my faith? All I ever heard from other believers was how faith in God was measured by our ability to keep our mental health stable and in check. It weighed so heavy on my mind I could not find peace. Confusion and suffering were my only companion and contributed to the endless shaking I could not break free from. I had to shed this confusion and move forward. I had to know the truth, the whole truth, and nothing but the truth on mental illness and its role in my life of faith. So, I picked up my Bible and started my own search for the truth. Through prayer and guidance from the holy spirit. This book is the outcome. No longer do I have to suffer with the confusion of how mental health plays a role in my life and if it was because I lacked faith in God. No longer do I have to wonder if my mental health was a punishment for lack of faith. No longer do I have to wonder if the pills I take and skills I have learned would condemn me in Gods eyes. I have answers that have helped me and brought me peace and I feel blessed to share them with you. My hope is you can find the strength to let go of false beliefs you have heard and may have took to heart and find peace in the what God's word says.

Knowledge is Power

Proverbs 24:5 A wise man [is] strong; yea, a man of knowledge increaseth strength.

Proverbs 8:10 Receive my instruction, and not silver; and knowledge rather than choice gold.

Hosea 4:6 My people are destroyed for lack of knowledge

How are you today? The pressure to answer this question on any given day with complete truth all depends on who is asking. Most of the time I've found myself saying "I'm fine" and then will move on to another subject. Mainly because if I was to tell the truth then the reaction may not be a good one. I just couldn't handle another negative reaction (or so I thought). I have been told on many occasions that my anxiety and depression are something that can be controlled. That we each have the ability to reach into our souls and clean up our internal houses; the lack of doing so is anxiety, depression, or another mental struggle. That this is my fault. I would say that a person who has maybe three or four panic episodes in their lifetime or who experiences depression for a period of time after the loss of a loved one this is true. They grieve their loss. They panic when their child has an allergic reaction to peanuts. They experience the so-called "normal" level of anxiety and depression that a person has. They get themselves under control in a timely manner and go on with life. This may be normal for the majority of people in this world, but what about the minority?

Anxiety (Panic Disorder), Depression (Major Depression Disorder), and CPTSD (Complex Post Traumatic Stress Disorder) for me have felt as though I have a burden around my shoulders that is ever constant and nagging. It can feel like a great struggle to move in any direction. Or something to be ashamed of because the only ones who understand, or are accepting, are the ones who have gone through it. The constant fear of judgement and pressure from others to live a certain way because their view does not allow them to see anything else. The overwhelming fear of failure in a given minute that leaves me stuck in a behavioral pattern that gives me the most relief from my misery. The uncontrollable shaking, mind racing, extreme fatigue without sleep, or sleep without being able to motivate to get up and go, anger, hopelessness. Triggers, triggers everywhere! Noises, words, phrases, loud sounds, smells, thoughts, people, places, or even a picture triggers something in me that seems to take over my body without control and at any given minute. Sound familiar? Or maybe you know something is just not right and are unsure what it is. You don't feel anything, and you feel as though you are walking around in a hollowed shell. Your insecurities and lack of confidence keep you from stepping out and being honest. Or, your mind is so foggy you can't tell the difference from what part is you and what part is you trying to please others or be what others think you should be. Or, you are so frustrated and fed up that the anger welling up inside you never seems to go away and can be triggered at the slightest of things. The result of all or none of these statements can all be narrowed down to "I'm overwhelmed; it's hopeless; I'm out of control." I do not say all these things to make you feel this way, but in that it may help you see you are not the only one who does. Or, you may be a person who does not understand mental struggles and this can give you an idea of what is going on inside the person you love.

I am not writing this as a "do this" or "don't do that" and you will be just fine. I am writing this to help give you an understanding of how we are made, how our world works, a glimpse of how God sees us as we are, and how biblical beliefs can play a role in mental struggle. I am a true believer of God and His written word. I believe that His written word, the bible, is a tool of help, warnings, understanding, knowledge, and love. NOT AN EXTENDED LIST OF DOS AND DO NOTS OR SHOULDS AND SHOULD NOTS. Knowledge is power!! Knowledge gives us the ability to get unstuck where we lay and move forward with confidence and help. Let's explore God's word and gain some knowledge on mental struggles

HELPFUL BIBLE INFORMATION IN ORDER TO MOVE FORWARD

The Bible makes things very clear and easy to understand; it's just a matter of digging up the information. To help us on this journey there is something of great importance we need to understand about the Bible. The Bible is not meant to be taken one verse at a time, but in its entirety. As a whole.

> **_2 Timothy 3:16_** *All scripture is given by inspiration of God, and is profitable for doctrine, for reproof, for correction, for instruction in <u>righteousness </u>(equity of character).*

> **<u>Psalm 19:7</u>** *The law of the Lord is <u>perfect</u> (complete), converting the soul: the testimony of the Lord is sure, making wise the simple.*

> **<u>Revelation 21:5</u>** *And he that sat upon the throne said, Behold, I make all things new. And he said unto me, write: for these words are true and faithful.*

> **<u>Romans 15:4</u>** *For whatsoever things were written aforetime were written for our learning, that we through patience and comfort of scripture might have hope.*

Yes! It is very complicated to find what we often need but there is a great process that works well. When something in the Bible is to be taken literally you will find that it is repeated. The key is, what pastors learn in seminary school, to take more than one set of scriptures on a subject <u>from across the Bible</u> and put them together to tell the whole story. Yes! It requires work, but the results are awesome!! Let me emphasize <u>scriptures, not verses.</u> Look at the verse in context, study the lesson or story going on and the different words used. By doing this it allows us the whole truth and nothing but the truth and Satan cannot get a foothold in trying to persuade us otherwise.

> **<u>2 Peter 1:20-21</u>** *We have also a more sure word of prophecy; whereunto ye do well that ye take heed, as unto a light that shineth in a dark place, until the day dawn, and the day star arise in your hearts: Knowing this first, that no prophecy of the scripture is of any private interpretation. For the prophecy came not in old time by the will of man: but holy men of God spake as they were moved by the Holy Ghost.*

__John 17:17__ Sanctify them through thy truth: thy word is truth.

__Revelations 22:18__ For I testify unto every man that heareth the words of the prophecy of this book…

__2 Timothy 2:15__ Study to shew thyself approved unto God, a workman that needeth not to be ashamed, rightly dividing word of truth.

One of my biggest struggles have been those who have misquoted or misused the Bible to influence me. This used to leave me very confused and in constant turmoil. Well, God is not the author of confusion.

__1 Corinthians 14:33__ For God is not the author of confusion, but of peace, as in all churches of the saints.

__John 10:10__ The thief cometh not, but for to steal, and to kill, and to destroy: I am come that they might have life, and that they might have it more abundantly.

__James 3:16-17__ For where envying and strife is, there is confusion and every evil work. But wisdom that is from above is first pure, then peaceable, gentle, and easy to be intreated, full of mercy and good fruits, and without partiality, and without hypocrisy.

When we are confused, stuck, or struggling, we need to make a change. Be open minded to change and grow your beliefs. This change comes from moving forward, finding the truth, for the truth will set us free!

> **Hosea 4:6** *My people are destroyed for lack of knowledge: …*
>
> **1 Corinthians 15:57** *The sting of death is sin; and the strength of sin is the law. But thanks be to God, which giveth us victory through our Lord Jesus Christ.*
>
> **John 8:31-32** *Then said Jesus to those Jews which believed on Him, if ye continue in my word, then are ye my disciples indeed; And ye shall know the truth, and the truth shall make you free.*
>
> **Hebrews 4:12** *For the word of God [is] quick, and powerful, and sharper than any two-edged sword, piercing even to the dividing asunder of soul and spirit, and of the joints and marrow, and [is] a discerner of the thoughts and intents of the heart.*

Avoid sources that cannot give you multiple scriptures on a subject. As we move forward, I will always provide more than one verse or set of scripture for you. Look up the scriptures and see how they relate. Mark them in your Bible so they will be easier to find, because they will be ones you will need to be constantly reaffirmed of when a bad day is eminent. Your mind is not meant to memorize and hold all this info. Let go of the pressure to have everything perfect, to know everything, to take on everything. Your body is not designed to have all the answers nor is it designed to take on the entire knowledge of the Bible. Knowledge comes gradually! By studying with intent, by praying with intent, and by letting God have control of your heart and mind. He will give you the answers when He wants you to have them. So, take a deep breath and be good to yourself, rejoice in the fact that you are willing to learn and grow for that is all God asks of you!! He will reveal the mysteries of His Kingdom as you seek it. They do not come to you upon salvation.

> **_Deuteronomy 4:29_** *But if from thence thou shalt seek the Lord thy God, thou shalt find him, if thou seek him with all thy heart and with all thy soul.*

> **_Proverbs 8:17_** *I love them that love me; and those that seek me early shall find me.*

> **_Proverbs 14:6_** *A scorner seeketh wisdom, and findeth it not: but knowledge is easy unto him that understandeth.*

> **_Jeremiah 29:13_** *And ye shall seek me, and find me, when ye shall search for me with all your heart.*

> **_Matthew 7:7-8_** *Ask, and it shall be given you; seek and ye shall find; knock and it shall be opened unto you: For everyone that asketh receiveth; and he that seeketh findeth; and to him that knocketh it shall be opened.*

Next, be aware that the majority of words have more than one definition that is not constrained by the English language. The original Bible was written in portions with Hebrew, Aramaic, and Greek. The span of time from the writings of the Bible until now make it difficult to understand the definition of terms. So, as you are reading God's word be aware some words may be different in context than our current usage. Or, it may have more than one definition and the definition differs due the context in which it is used. For example:

Temptations

English language: A strong urge or desire to do something that may be unwise. A sin.

Hebrew language: A test or trial, proving.

Explained more in the chapter titled, "The Yoke"

Charity

English language: The giving of possessions to help others in need. An organization set up to help those in need.

Hebrew language: Brotherly love, affection, goodwill, love, benevolence. A love feasts.

Explained more in the chapter titled, "The Masters"

Perfect

English Language: Without cause for blame, shame, or guilt. Without mistakes.

Hebrew language: Complete, whole, entire, sound, strengthen, to make one what he ought to be, bring to an end. Reaching your full potential, your completeness to the end of this life, maturity.

Explained more in the chapter titled, "The Yoke"

Good or Right

English Language: a list of things that are considered right or proper or traditional way of acting.

Hebrew Language: character of doing without the purpose of appearance or use to grow stature.

Explained more in the chapter titled, "Freedom in the Light"

Bad or Wrong

English Language: A list of things that are considered wrong and not a traditional way of acting.

Hebrew Language: Character of doing for the purpose of growing in stature or appearance.

Explained more in the chapter titled, "The Oxen"

To help with this, I use an app called My Sword Bible for Android or Pocketsword for iphone. Not only can you search for specific words, phrases, and translations, but the app also has a number after each word you can click on and it will give you the Hebrew definition used by Strong's dictionary in that context. It is awesome!! I stick to the original KJV and use the app to help with words and have found that many translations try to narrow in the definition for you by their interpretation. I have also found they use inappropriate words or take portions of the verses out, and I'm not very comfortable with that. I want the truth, the whole truth and let the Holy Spirit guide my knowledge. Another truth I have used is the King James Bible. I am not discrediting other translations, but be aware that other translations are not as close. The translation of a received text (including KJV) is within 5% of the original. Those translations known from the critical text makes over 6,000 changes, including changing words, omitting words, omitting verses, and changes in doctrine. Within these translations they contradict themselves throughout the Bible, making their percentage of accuracy less than 5%.

The next step to understanding the Bible is the heart to seek. Matthew 13 speaks about the mysteries of the kingdom. These mysteries are written in parables. This I never really understood. Why write in riddles and not in plain understanding ways? The reason for this? Matthew 13: 1-23, (Explained in the chapter titled, "Parable of the Sower.") God did this for those who really wanted to know the answers could find them. If a person sought the truth, searched it out, studied it, took time to pray about it, and took fellowship with others searching for the same, then they would find it. But for those who had no heart in it, only pursued it half-heartedly, didn't have their heart in the right place to accept the answer, well then, they wouldn't understand. I have often found myself getting confused and aggravated with God and His ways. Why does He not just give me the understanding? Why does it take so much to comprehend what His word is telling me at times? Because that is just the way it is. Constantly questioning this process will not get you anywhere. Constantly questioning our circumstances does not get us anywhere. It leaves us stuck and unable to move forward. This process is here to show us that with true dedication from the heart we can gain the knowledge needed to move forward. If we make the effort, ask for help, face our frustrated self, and push through the hard stuff we WILL find the answers. Asking for help allows God to be our victor, not ourselves. I was blind but now I see! So, before we move forward. Make sure your heart is in it! Believe, repent, pray, and read your Bible daily! Have a support system. Church family, prayer group, bible study group, psychologist, psychiatrists, meds if needed. Make a conscious effort to want to know more! BE OPEN -MINDED!!! Being open is not a way of letting the devil in to influence you, but to let God change you and grow you!!! To want to get better and grow and learn from this. If you get stuck or confused or disagree, keep going until you reach the end! Quitting will only leave you where you started! Also, I am a music nut! I love music and I find peace and help with music when I am at my worst. Throughout this study I may provide songs that might help with your understanding. Music has great power of expressions and feelings. To have a playlist to play as a reminder of what you know in your heart until your mind catches up is refreshing and has the ability to build your confidence in what you believe.

THIS IS NOT JUST FOR THOSE WHO ARE OPENLY STRUGGLING!! THIS IS FOR EVERYONE, EVERY BELIEVER AND NON-BELIEVER, BECAUSE WE ALL STRUGGLE AND CAN LEARN FROM IT!!

Knowledge is Power, but it takes time, effort, and commitment!!

The Struggle Defined

The struggle is clear to us that live in the daily grind of searching for happiness. I am not happy when my anxiety is overwhelming or my depression is consuming. My mind is at a constant battle. The fight for daily survival comes to the front of my mind and consumes every move, thought, action, and feeling. I am a slave to it. Slavery is the condition where one is owned by another. The owner tells the slave when they can eat, sleep, work, and play. I feel as though my anxiety and depression has placed me in the position of being a slave, and the anxiety and depression is my owner. It tells me when to eat, when to sleep, when to work, and when to play. Again, does this sound familiar to you? Or do you have a loved one in your life that acts as though they are trapped? They constantly cancel on you in the last minute, get upset when you constantly confront them with expectations. Easy to anger. Easy to hurt their feelings. Mood changes on a dime. Nausea and can't eat, tired but can't sleep. The littlest of jobs is presented to them and they are instantly overwhelmed. A slave to something you can't see and don't comprehend how they can act or behave the way that they do. They are okay with their normal routine, but add something or a few things to it and they shut you off or back away. Trust me the struggle is so real. The picture that is painted within their mind is so fierce it would even scare you. So fierce they can't explain it to you on any terms. They have an invisible yoke of bondage around their neck, hooked to chains that control when to move to the right or left, when to stop and go.

This is the picture I paint for you and this is how I am going to explain mental struggles going forward. Slave, yoke, bondage, control. This brings to my mind a picture of a pair of oxen with a yoke around their neck. Plowing into the earth, with their master behind them directing them. Each part in this picture plays a role within the job that lies before them. The oxen are the man power; the ground is the work field that needs turned for planting; the masters are the leaders/teachers; the yoke is the bondage. Yet the oxen are free within this scenario! They are content. But how?

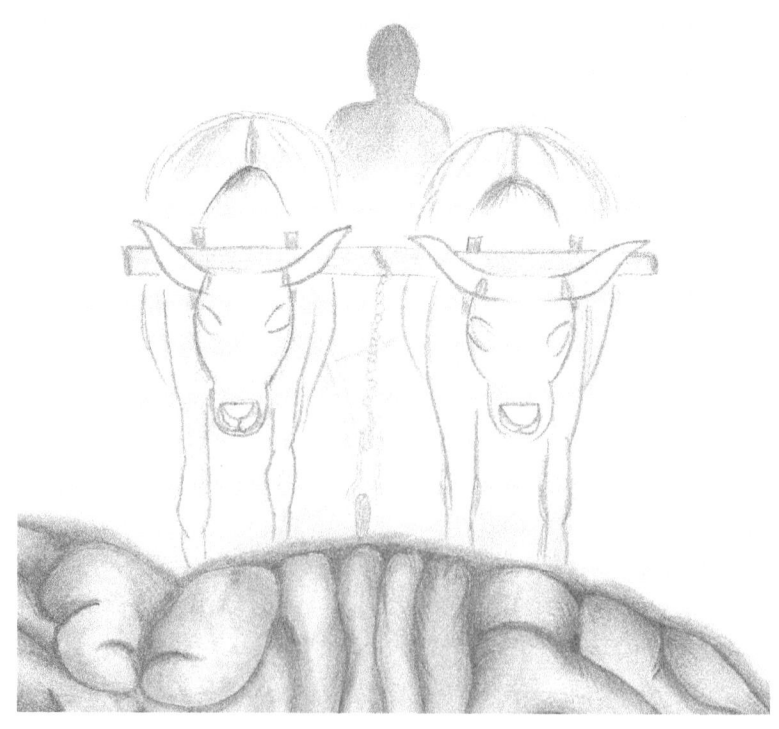

The Work Field

Ephesians 6:12 *"For we wrestle not against <u>Flesh and blood</u> (our human bodies) but against <u>principalities</u> (magistracy of angels and demons, original rulers) against <u>powers</u> (the state to which one is free to choose, this choice is decided in the mind. Mental powers) against <u>rulers of darkness of this world</u> (Satan and His demons) against <u>spiritual</u> wickedness in high places."* (rational soul or spirit, thought out mind, heart of our existence)

2 Corinthians 10:3-5 *"For though we walk in the flesh we do not war after the flesh. For the weapons of our warfare are not <u>carnal</u> (flesh and blood), but mighty through God to the pulling down of strongholds. Casting down <u>imaginations</u> (thoughts) and every high thing that exalteth itself against the <u>Knowledge of God</u> (truth of your existence, your struggles, your mortality, your faith in Him) and bringing into <u>captivity</u> (to capture one's mind, captivate, hold from distraction) every thought to the obedience of Christ."*

Romans 8:5-8 *"For they that are after the <u>Flesh</u> (carnally minded, selfish, wants, desires, cravings) do mind the things of the flesh; but they that are after the spirit (character, values, morals, beliefs) the things of the spirit. For to be carnally minded is death but to be spiritually minded is life and peace. Because the carnal mind is* *enmity against God: for it is not subject to the Law of God neither indeed can be so then they that are in the flesh cannot please God.*

These verses clearly define the battle between two forces or what I will call the work field with two masters: The carnal mind and the spiritual mind. So, let's clearly define them with the words and verses above.

> **Carnal minded**- flesh and blood, physical ailments, wants, cravings, desires, fantasy, foolish.

> **Spiritual minded**- values, beliefs, rational soul, realistic, wise, character, contentment (acceptance).

These verses clearly state the work field we face every day takes place in the mind. The mind can be centered around what the body needs, wants, and desires, or we can re-center our mind on the things that hold value like our character traits, morals, values, and beliefs. When we get lost in the wants and needs, we will often find that our struggles with the desire to avoid pain, struggle, hard times, and trauma, become a constant desire to feel safe and secure and happy. Do we not all strive every day to be happy and peaceful at all cost? Isn't this why some use alcohol and drugs to relax and slow down to gain a moment of peace and happiness? To escape the daily trials of the mind? Even those with ADD or ADHD. The mind never rests and is in constant go mode. Even the racing mind that never rests and is always dreaming. I believe this is why when we are in constant "work mode" then we are able to avoid the dark thoughts and fears that plague us. Sometimes, we even cut ourselves, or flourish with physical pain because it gives us a break from the emotional pain that overwhelms us. Eventually our bodies become exhausted from the load and we are forced to slow down. Or on the other hand our depression makes us desire to just lay down and sleep and escape. The overwhelming desire to despise getting up and getting involved. All of this is SOOO hard! Yet, it is manageable!!

These verses show us that the struggle is real and that it is real for everyone. I often doubt with the struggle I face every day, thinking I have done something wrong to be given this struggle. Yet these verses show how everyone faces these struggles. It is what it is. These struggles just come in different sizes. Those of us who have faced trauma, abuse, neglect, and/or health issues are more susceptible to anxiety and depression or other mental struggles. Also, those who have a genetic disposition can no sooner avoid or escape the fate of experiencing the overwhelming emotions of anxiety, depression, or other mental struggles. These factors make us more vulnerable, but it also opens up a door for us to experience the power of God.

> *2 Corinthians 12:9-10 And he said unto me, my grace is sufficient for thee for my strength is made perfect in weakness. Most gladly therefore will I rather glory in my infirmities, that the power of Christ may rest upon me. Therefore, I take pleasure in infirmities, in reproaches, in necessities, in persecutions, in distresses for Christ's sake: for when I am weak, then am I strong.*

God's power is made strongest within our weakness. When we are at our lowest, we find that we can no longer do it ourselves. However, we keep trying to handle the situation, take control, work at it, change this, or try that. When we are in this state, we fail to look to God for help, but solely depend on ourselves. It is when we finally see and can confess that we cannot do this alone, relying on God is when His power can be presented. The only thing standing in our way is ourselves. We spend our days plowing at our minds to make things fit in perfect rows, place our feelings in perfect order, or trying to plow others minds to think and see how we do. When we do that, we lose sight of everything and become overwhelmed. It is not about controlling the desires, but about acknowledging you have them, accepting them as part of who you are, and learning from it. Our minds are not designed to be in perfect rows, but in a beautiful chaos of twists and turns. God's personal design. Perfect defined in the Bible is to be complete and whole. This can be obtained through chaos with acknowledgement and acceptance. Once we acknowledge and accept it, we can move forward and grow from it. One day at a time.

To better understand the work field, let's take a look at its origin and grow knowledge from it. How does the Bible explain the origin of the work field in the mind?

Music

("King of My Heart" by Love & the Outcome)

("Rise" by Katy Perry)

("Beautiful" by Francesca Battistelli)

("Drops in The Ocean" by Hawk Nelson)

("Walk on Water" by Britt Nicole)

("No Matter What" by Papa Roach)

("Beautiful Messes" by Hillary Scott and the Scott Family)

The Oxen

THE ORIGIN OF THE WORK FIELD

Genesis 2:8-9, 15-17 *"And the Lord God planted a garden eastward in Eden; and there he put the man whom he had formed. And out of the ground made the Lord God to grow every tree that is pleasant to the sight, and good for food;* <u>the tree of life</u> *(mortality) also in the midst of the garden,* <u>and the tree of knowledge of good</u> <u>and evil</u> *(*intellectual nature that is pleasant and prosperous and also the vicious nature that is malignant and generates calamity). And the Lord God took the man, and put him into the garden of Eden to dress it and to keep it. And the Lord God commanded the man, saying, of every tree of the garden thou mayest freely eat: But of the tree of knowledge of good and evil, thou shalt not eat of it: for in the day that thou eatest thereof thou shalt surely die.*

Genesis 3:1-7 *"Now the* <u>serpent was more subtil</u> *(cunning, smart, deceptive) than any beast of the field which the Lord God has made. And he said unto the woman, Yea, hath God said, Ye shall not eat of every tree of the garden? And the woman said unto the serpent, we may eat of the fruit of the trees of the garden: But the fruit of the tree is in the midst of the garden, God hath said, Ye shall not eat of it, neither shall ye touch it,* <u>lest ye</u> <u>die</u> *(physical death). And the serpent said unto the woman, Ye shall not surely die. For God doth know that in the day ye eat*

21

thereof, then <u>your eyes shall be opened</u> (your mind open to more knowledge), and ye shall be as gods, knowing good and evil. And when the woman saw that the tree was good for food, and that it was pleasant to the eyes, and <u>a tree to be desired to make one wise</u> (increase knowledge). She took of the fruit thereof, and did eat, and gave also unto her husband with her; and he did eat. And the <u>eyes of them both were opened</u> (received an increase of knowledge of both good and evil), and they knew they were naked; and they sewed fig leaves together, and made themselves aprons."

I think the key word here that is repeated is knowledge. Let's take a deeper look at it. First, Adam and Eve at the time of creation only had knowledge of good. A goodness about them (good in the bible is defined as not a list of things that are considered right or proper way of acting, but the character of doing without the purpose of appearance or use). They had no awareness, experience, acquaintance, intelligence of evil or bad, or of acting in order to place appearance upon their stature. They were <u>created</u> in the image of God (Genesis 1:26-27). God being the fair God that He was gave them the options. He gave them direction to not eat of the tree of knowledge of good and evil lest they die. What we need to realize here is those created by God did not die a physical death. Those created were in the goodness and likeness of God. Perfect, sinless beings with only the knowledge, actions, and heart of goodness. *Genesis 2:25 "And they were both naked, the man and his wife, and were not ashamed."* They did not have an understanding yet of shame!

When Adam and Eve ate from the fruit of the tree of knowledge of good and evil it opened up their mind and heart to emotional knowledge, or an intellectual nature that is pleasant and prosperous, as well as the vicious nature that is malignant and generates calamity. An exposure to two entities that exist that are opposed or opposite one from another and that are the worst of all to experience. What do I mean by experience…let's take a look?

> ***Genesis 3:7-13*** *"And the eyes of them both were opened, and they <u>knew</u> that they were naked; and they sewed fig leaves together and made themselves aprons. And they heard the voice of the Lord God walking in the garden in the cool of the day; and Adam and his wife <u>hid</u> themselves from the presence of the Lord God amongst the trees of the garden. And the Lord God called unto Adam, and said unto him, Where art thou? And he said, I heard thy voice in the garden and I was <u>afraid</u>, because I was naked; and I hid myself. And he said, who told thee that thou were naked? Hast thou eaten of the tree, whereof I commanded thee that thou shouldest not eat? And the man said, <u>the woman whom thou gavest to be with me, she gave me of the tree, and I did eat.</u> And the Lord God said unto the woman, what is this that thou have done? And the woman said <u>the serpent beguiled me, and I did eat.</u>*

These underlined keywords tell us what was in the hearts of Adam and Eve after their eyes were opened. They knew, hid, were afraid, and it was her fault, and the Serpent's fault. Do you see the pattern of negative actions, thoughts, and emotions? Avoidance, shame,

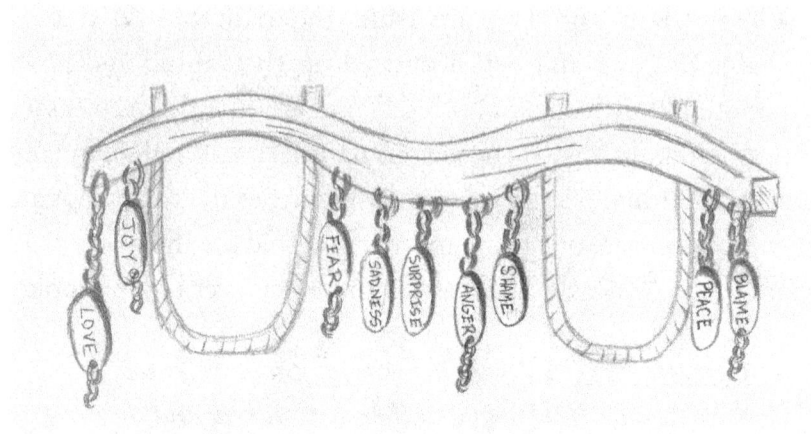

fear, blame, and pride. These are all attributes of the knowledge of evil. They did not have this knowledge before they ate the fruit but after. This is where our knowledge of evil comes from. The origin of the struggle of the mind takes its place among men. OUR YOKE! Having the ability to understand these negative emotions, experience them, and live with them.

We now have an origin to where this line of thinking comes from. It is not from our actions or something we have done. It's from the original sin that opened up our knowledge to the dark side of things. A state we each are born with. We are the oxen, pulling, struggling, wrestling through this life. Our yoke of bondage hanging around our necks is our daily struggles (thoughts, shame, blame, guilt, physical desire, lack of knowledge or understanding). You may have those in your life who live in denial that they do not have these struggles. You may be that person, constantly running from the truth. The fear of acknowledging these issues exist makes you an outsider, a crazy person, someone out of control, unacceptable, unlovable. The truth is we are all crazy, we are all outsiders, we are all out of control. Being born with the knowledge of good and evil places us in these categories. It is not something to be ashamed of. It is what it is. The most amazing thing is God loves us anyway. We live every day with the pressure and judgement of others; to hold ourselves to an imaginary level of goodness in order to be loved and accepted. But we lose sight of the fact that God loves us as we are. Or you may be the person who thinks that your belief in God gives you righteousness (perfect goodness). Goodness that keeps you from sinning and from having struggles. The belief that an invisible barrier overcomes you when you accept the Lord as your savior. This barrier protects you from all things bad and you are overcome with knowledge and have the ability to spot out who is saved and who is not. You stand on a pedestal and your faith allows you to see what is righteous and what is not. The belief salvation protects you from the world and its ways. The truth is that salvation (belief in God and His Son) does not get rid of the struggle and make you righteous. Salvation opens up the opportunity to have hope. Hope in an eternal resting place that is righteous, free from pain, suffering, and evil. Hope that you have a loving Father to help you in the daily struggles of this life as you go through it. Hope that God will use all these struggles to make you stronger and grows you in knowledge and truth. Hope that even though you may face a physical death it is not the end. Hope in His promise that your mental health issues are temporary.

God does not love and accept us because we are perfect. He loves and accepts us because we are not. Take for instance a bird. A bird flying around high in the sky is so beautiful and graceful. We love to watch them and listen to them sing. We enjoy taking our time in learning each and every one of them and knowing them by their different names. Then one comes along and flies into your window and it falls to the ground. The overwhelming sense of help and protection comes over you and you wish, hope, and pray that the little bird will be alright. You don't stop loving it because it made a mistake. On the contrary: you love it more for the struggle it is facing. You pick it up as carefully as possible and love and nurture it in hopes that it will fly away. This is how God loves us. Our mistakes and imperfections do not make us less lovable. Instead, it makes us more loveable. Our mistakes and imperfections allow us to have a relationship with God and those around us that is more deep and profound. The greater the struggle the greater the love. It forces us to dig down deep and explore ourselves. To see how committed we are to God and our loved ones. It is easy to love someone who never does anything wrong. To love someone who never makes you upset. But how much more love does it take to love those who have hurt you or those you don't understand. Or, to love a God that doesn't give you a perfect life. It requires effort and the effort makes the bond stronger.

> ***Luke 6:32-33*** *For if ye love them which love you, what thank have ye? for sinners also love those that love them. And if ye do good to them which do good to you, what thank have ye? for sinners also do even the same.*

__Matthew 5:45-48__ That ye may be the children of your Father which is in heaven: for the maketh his sun to rise on the evil and on the good, and sendeth rain on the just and on the unjust. For if ye love them which love you, what reward have ye? do not even the publicans the same? And if ye salute your brethren only, what do ye more than others? do not even the publicans so? Be ye therefore perfect, even as your Father which is in heaven is __perfect__. (not perfect as without mistakes, but perfect as reaching your full potential, your completeness to the end of this life, maturity)

The greatest thing you can do for yourself or your loved one is to love them. Regardless of stature, regardless of success and failure <u>as you see it.</u> Give yourself a break and love yourself. Love the hard stuff about you with the easy. Love that other person for the struggle they are facing and respect it. You don't have to agree with it or how they handle it. But respect the struggle and acknowledge it is there. The greatest thing anyone has done for me it to recognize the struggle I face every day, and to not place blame on me for it. To respect what I am going through and acknowledge its difficulty. Respect enables love and confidence and freedom to be one's self. Blames takes love away and makes one insecure and guarded.

Next, let's explore who the masters are. Who is guiding us and leading us in our daily lives and what does the Bible say about them and their character? If you wish to study more and dig deeper on original sin, check out the chapter, "Is God a fair God?" Our doubts of wondering if God is fair can keep us from completely believing and trusting in Him. See how God worked with Adam and Eve after their knowledge of good and evil came to them.

<u>Music</u>

("He Is with Us" by Love and the Outcome)
("More Than You Think I Am" by Danny Gokey)
("Issues" by Julia Michaels)
("Give Your Heart A Break" by Demi Lovato)

The Masters

Satan, dark

__Revelations 12:9__ And the great dragon was cast out, that old serpent, called the Devil, and Satan, which deceiveth the whole world: he was cast out into the earth, and his angels were cast out with him.

__Ezekiel 28:13-19__ Thou hast been in Eden the garden of God; every precious stone was thy covering, the sardius, topaz, and the diamond, the beryl, the onyx, and the jasper, the sapphire, the emerald, and the carbuncle, and gold: the workmanship of thy tabrets and of thy pipes was prepared in thee in the day that thou wast created. Thou art the anointed cherub that covereth; and I have set thee so: thou wast upon the holy mountain of God; thou hast walked up and down in the midst of the stones of fire. Thou wast perfect in thy ways from the day that thou wast created, till iniquity was found in thee. By the multitude of thy merchandise they have filled the midst of thee with violence, and thou hast sinned: therefore, I will cast thee as profane out of the mountain of God: and I will destroy thee, O covering cherub, from the midst of the stones of fire. Thine heart was lifted up because of thy *beauty, thou hast corrupted thy wisdom by reason of thy brightness: I will cast thee to the ground, I will lay thee before kings, that they may behold thee. Thou hast defiled thy sanctuaries by the multitude of thine iniquities, by the iniquity of thy traffick; therefore, will I bring forth a fire from the midst of thee, it shall devour thee, and I will bring thee to ashes upon the earth in the sight of all them that behold thee. All they that know thee among the people shall be astonished at thee: thou shalt be a terror, and never shalt thou be any more.*

Isaiah 14:12-17 *How art thou fallen from heaven, O Lucifer, son of the morning! how art thou cut down to the ground, which didst weaken the nations! For thou hast said in thine heart, I will ascend into heaven, I will exalt my throne above the stars of God: I will sit also upon the mount of the congregation, in the sides of the north: I will ascend above the heights of the clouds; I will be like the most High. Yet thou shalt be brought down to hell, to the sides of the pit. They that see thee shall narrowly look upon thee, and consider thee, saying, is this the man that made the earth to tremble, that did shake kingdoms; That made the world as a wilderness, and destroyed the cities thereof; that opened not the house of his prisoners?*

Luke 10:18 *And he said unto them, I beheld Satan as lightning fall from heaven.*

I Timothy 3:6 *Not a novice, lest being lifted up with pride he falls into the condemnation of the devil*

Revelations 20:2-3 *And he laid hold on the dragon, that old serpent, which is the Devil, and Satan, and bound him a thousand years, and cast him into the bottomless pit, and shut him up, and set a seal upon him, that he should deceive the nations no more, till the thousand years should be fulfilled: and after that he must be loosed a little season.*

Matthew 25:41 *Then shall he say also unto them on the left hand, depart from me, ye cursed, into everlasting fire, prepared for the devil and his angels:*

Job 1:6-12 *Now there was a day when the sons of God came to present themselves before the LORD, and Satan came also among them. And the LORD said unto Satan, Whence comest thou? Then Satan answered the LORD, and said, from going to and fro in the earth, and from walking up and down in it. And the LORD said unto Satan, Hast thou considered my servant Job, that there is none like him in the earth, a perfect and an upright man, one that feareth God, and escheweth evil? Then Satan answered the LORD, and said, Doth Job fear God for nought? Hast not thou made a hedge about him, and about his house, and about all that he hath on every side? thou hast blessed the work of his hands, and his substance is increased in the land. But put forth thine hand now, and touch all that he hath, and he will curse thee to thy face. And the LORD said unto Satan, Behold, all that he hath is in thy power; only upon himself put not forth thine hand. So, Satan went forth from the presence of the LORD*

__2 Corinthians 11:14__ And no marvel; for Satan himself is transformed into an angel of light.

__Marks 1:13__ And he was there in the wilderness forty days, tempted of Satan; and was with the wild beasts; and the angels ministered unto him

__Revelations 12:7__ And there was war in heaven: Michael and his angels fought against the dragon; and the dragon fought and his angels,

__1 Peter 5:8__ Be sober, be vigilant; because your adversary the devil, as a roaring lion, walketh about, seeking whom he may devour:

__John 10:10__ The thief cometh not, but for to steal, and to kill, and to destroy: I am come that they might have life, and that they might have it more abundantly.

__John 8:44__ Ye are of your father the devil, and the lusts of your father ye will do. He was a murderer from the beginning, and abode not in the truth, because there is no truth in him. When he speaketh a lie, he speaketh of his own: for he is a liar, and the father of it.

__Matthew 13:19__ When any one heareth the word of the kingdom, and understandeth it not, then cometh the wicked one, and catcheth away that which was sown in his heart. This is he which received seed by the way side

__1 John 5:19__ And we know that we are of God, and the whole world lieth in wickedness. World

John 12:31 *Now is the judgment of this world: now shall the prince of this world be cast out.*

Job 1:12 *And the LORD said unto Satan, Behold, all that he hath is in thy power; only upon himself put not forth thine hand. So, Satan went forth from the presence of the LORD.*

2 Corinthians 12:7 *And lest I should be exalted above measure through the abundance of the revelations, there was given to me a thorn in the flesh, the messenger of Satan to buffet me, lest I should be exalted above measure.*

Ephesians 2:*2 Wherein in time past ye walked according to the course of this world, according to the prince of the power of the air, the spirit that now worketh in the children of disobedience*

2 Timothy 2:26 *And that they may recover themselves out of the snare of the devil, who are taken captive by him at his will*

Acts 26:18 *To open their eyes, and to turn them from darkness to light, and from the power of Satan unto God, that they may receive forgiveness of sins, and inheritance among them which are sanctified by faith that is in me their eyes so that they may turn from darkness to light and from the dominion of Satan to God, that they may receive forgiveness of sins and an inheritance among those who have been sanctified by faith in Me.'*

What we now know about Satan is he was once an angel, created by God, cast out of heaven with followers. He thought himself to be better than God and took measures to secure himself on the throne and it failed to happen. He was cast out unto the earth with his angels as a spirit. The same earth Adam and Eve were created and placed upon. Satan presented himself to Eve as the beautiful serpent. Satan strategically asked, questioned, and presented opinions to get Eve to doubt the truth of God. Satan is the prince of the air of this world and his power is strong here. The only power he cannot have is over one's soul. This power remains with each individual to choose what happens to their soul, through belief or unbelief. Satan's persuasion can hold unbeliever's captive to his ways and desires. Those who have chosen to believe in God and His sacrifice of His Son for our sins/sinful nature are still affected by Satan and his dark ways. Satan sole purpose is to seek, destroy, steal, and kill. He is known as Lucifer, Legion, Angel of Mourning, Devil, Satan, Serpent, Darkness, and Dragon. He comes to us in forms of an angel of light, appearing as something of hope and joy and beauty. He places thoughts of doubt and makes is appear as hope. He encourages us to jump out on our own and makes us believe that we need no one and nothing. He is the master of evil and darkness and encourages us to live by the demands of our flesh. *Romans 8:13 "For if ye live after the flesh, ye shall die: but if ye through the Spirit do mortify the deeds of the body, ye shall live."*

Light, God –

> *1 Corinthians 10:13 There hath no temptation taken you but such as is common to man: but God is faithful, who will not suffer you to be tempted above*

that ye are able; but will with the temptation also make a way to escape, that ye may be able to bear it.

James 4:6 *But he giveth more grace. Wherefore he saith, God resisteth the proud, but giveth grace unto the humble.*

John 3:16 *For God so loved the world, that he gave his only begotten Son, that whosoever believeth in him should not perish, but have everlasting life.*

1 Peter 2:9 *But ye are a chosen generation, a royal priesthood, a holy nation, a peculiar people; that ye should shew forth the praises of him who hath called you out of darkness into his marvellous light:*

2 Peter 3:9 *The Lord is not slack concerning his promise, as some men count slackness; but is longsuffering toward us, not willing that any should perish, but that all should come to repentance.*

1 John 4:8 *He that loveth not knoweth not God; for God is love*

Luke 22:43 *And there appeared an angel unto him from heaven, strengthening him.*

1 John 1:5 *This then is the message which we have heard of him, and declare unto you, that God is light, and in him is no darkness at all.*

Psalm 30:5 *For his anger endureth but a moment; in his favour is life: weeping may endure for a night, but joy cometh in the morning*

James 1:17 *Every* <u>*good*</u> *(useful, pleasant, agreeable) gift and every perfect gift is from above, and cometh down from the Father of lights, with whom is no variableness, neither shadow of turning.*

John 14:26 *But the Comforter, which is the Holy Ghost, whom the Father will send in my name, he shall teach you all things, and bring all things to your remembrance, whatsoever I have said unto you*

Isaiah 41:10 *Fear thou not; for I am with thee: be not dismayed; for I am thy God: I will strengthen thee; yea, I will help thee; yea, I will uphold thee with the right hand of my righteousness.*

James 4:7 *Submit yourselves therefore to God. Resist the devil, and he will flee from you*

Colossians 1:13 *Who hath delivered us from the power of darkness, and hath translated us into the kingdom of his dear Son*

Acts 26:18 *to open their eyes so that they may turn from darkness to light and from the dominion of Satan to God, that they may receive forgiveness of sins and an inheritance among those who have been sanctified by faith in Me*

Proverbs 3: 5-6 *Trust in the Lord with all thine heart, and lean not unto thy own understanding. In all they ways acknowledge Him and He shall direct thy path.*

__1 Peter 5:10__ After you have suffered a little while the God of all grace, who has called you to His own eternal glory in Christ Jesus, will himself complete and make you what you ought to be, establish and ground you securely, and strengthen and settle you.

__Psalm 58:11__ So that a man shall say, verily there is a reward for the righteous: verily he is a God that judgeth in the earth

__John 14:2__ In my Father's house are many mansions: if it were not so, I would have told you. I go to prepare a place for you, and if I go to prepare a place for you, I will come again and receive you unto myself, that where I am there ye may be also.

We find here a big difference from Satan's verses. God is for us not against us. God provides us a way to maneuver through this world of its temptations and trials and struggles. He sent His son as a sacrifice for our sins. He promises life and life more abundantly if we follow and trust in Him to direct our path. He will strengthen us, hold us close, send us a comforter, rescue us from darkness, and give us power to resist the devil. God is love and light and his anger is but for a moment. When we are His, we are His. There is nothing that can take us from the love of Christ or His protection. He promises if we look to Him, He will make all the sad and dark things we experience turn for our growth and benefit us in some way. When our life on earth is complete, He will raise us up to be with him in glory and live forever without pain, fear, and sorrow. Reward us for our pure hearts we have by accepting and trusting in him and give us a mansion. The true character of God is wrapped up in one word and that is love also known as charity.

> **I Corinthians 13:4-8** *"Charity suffereth long, and is kind; charity envieth not; charity vaunteth not itself, is not puffed up, doth not behave itself unseemly, seeketh not her own, is not easily provoked, thinketh no evil; Rejoiceth not in iniquity, but rejoiceth in truth; Beareth all things, believeth all things, hopeth all things, endureth all things. Charity never faileth;"*

God does not seek His happiness, but ours. The ultimate happiness is to come when we enter into heaven to be with our Lord. His sons sacrifice on the cross opened up that door. Jesus himself experienced temptation, suffering, depression, anxiety, anger, sorrow, despair, hopelessness, and, eventually, acceptance. Check out the chapter "Jesus life on earth".

This world has two masters. Each one would love the chance to get to know you, but each one's motives for getting to know you are different. The reality is we are born already subjected to these masters, but our intelligence of the matter is not yet developed. As we develop our intelligence, we become more aware of each master and their purpose. God's goal is for a lasting relationship, of friendship, trust, growth, and peace. Satan's goal is to keep you distracted from all things prosperous and envelope you into a state of confusion, pain, doubt, and fear. To keep you from any knowledge of God and hope you may have in Him. God will use your circumstance to make you stronger; Satan will use them to make you defeated. God's power is magnified with faith, growth, and prayer. Satan's power is magnified with doubt, stagnation, and rejection/avoidance. The most important fact is to realize you have a daily choice to recognize these masters and their forces around you.

P.S. One thing to remember is your belief in God does not exempt you from sin or being tempted by sin. Your belief in God gives you hope over sin. Hard times will still come, illness, struggle, tough relationships, and mean people. All of these things will still exist in this world. But God will help you as you experience and work through them. Not around them, but through! He gives the promise that the struggles are only temporary. Sometimes temporary on earth, or temporary until we see Him. There is great power in hope! What are you placing your hope upon?

Music

("Shake It Off" by Glee)
("Tornado" by Little Big Town)
("Broken" by Lindsey Haun)
("Stand by You" by Rachel Platten)

The Yoke

Galatians 6:5 "For every man shall bear his own burden."

Matthew 11: 28-30 "Come unto me all ye that labour and are heavy laden, and I will give you rest. Take my yoke upon you, and learn from me; for I am meek and lowly in heart; and ye shall find rest unto your souls. For my yoke is easy, and my burden is light."

What is a yoke? A yoke is 1) a wooden beam between a pair of animals to enable them to pull together a load when working; 2) metaphorically, used of any burden or bondage; 3) as that of slavery; 4) a balance, pair of scales; and 5) troublesome laws imposed on one.

We have been looking at the wooden beam between two animals to enable them to pull together a load when working. But let's add the others to it also.

1. **What is your yoke?**
2. **What do you feel like you're a slave to?**
3. **What is in balance or out of balance for you?**
4. **What troublesome laws or expectations do you have on your shoulders that are keeping you from moving forward?**

Get your highlighter and pen ready and, as you read, highlight those things you may relate to. Make a list of things you already know about yourself. If you're unsure, put a question mark beside it and move on.

1. What is your yoke? I would say after the reading of God's word and the studying we have done there are a few things that stand out. First would be our yoke of sin that we are burdened with from birth. I've recently been watching the series *Once Upon a Time.* The mixture of all our favorite fairy tales coming together in a kaleidoscope of relationships and adventure. They all have one thing in common: every character has a heart. They show this literally by the characters who possess great magic having the ability to pull anyone's heart from their chest. It does not kill them unless the heart is crushed. This gives them the ability to control or protect whoever has possession of that heart. What stands out to me is the villains have a dark, black heart and the heroes have a bright, red heart. Snow White, the main character, had a perfectly pure bright heart, because she was a hero who acted on behalf of others and sacrificed herself at all cost; she was completely selfless. Until she killed Cora the evil mother. When her heart was removed from her it possessed a black spot, the presence of darkness from that murder. Her heart that was once pure now is corrupted. It shows Snow White as being born a pure person with a pure heart. She spends her days acting pure because she was born pure. For us in reality we are the opposite. When we are born our heart is already corrupted with black, dark sin. We have the knowledge of darkness. Just look at any two or three-year-old and we will all swear that they are possessed by some dark spirit. One minute they are sweet as pie and then the next, they are throwing things, pitching a fit, and demanding to have their own way. Evidence that we are all born with a knowledge of darkness. As we grow, we learn the difference between light and dark. The path they each lead to and the decisions we will have to make to overcome. We spend our lives either drowning in darkness or overcoming in light. This is our constant yoke. Our work fields. Our battle.

> ***1 John 1:8-10*** - *If we say that we have no sin, we deceive ourselves, and the truth is not in us.*

> ***Romans 3:23*** - *For all have sinned, and come short of the glory of God;*

Other yokes we carry are those that make each one of us unique and different from each other. We each have our own weakness in different degrees. We can be weak in our beliefs and values, weak in our knowledge and understanding, weak in our body and health, weak in self-control of our desires. Most assuredly, our weakness will become apparent as we experience struggles.

> ***Psalm 73:26*** *My flesh and my heart faileth: but God is the strength of my heart, and my portion forever.*

> ***2 Corinthians 12:5-6*** *Of such an one will I glory: yet of myself I will not glory, but in mine infirmities. For though I would desire to glory, I shall not be a fool; for I will say the truth: but now I forbear, lest any man should think of me above that which he seeth me to be, or that he heareth of me.*

Other yokes are our temptations. Temptation is defined as a trial, a proving of one's beliefs and character, the internal struggle to fulfill the desires of the flesh, trouble. Again, be aware that every time you see temptation in the Bible it may not be defined as an internal struggle to fulfil the desires of the flesh. It more than likely will be the proving of one's beliefs or a trial of the strength of your beliefs. You may be stuck in a position to see if you will walk the walk or if you just talk the talk. Everyone's beliefs and values are different and come in different degrees. So, no one's temptations will come in equal measure.

> ***Matthew 6:13 and Luke 22:28*** *"Lead us not into temptation but deliver us from evil (darkness)"*
>
> ***Matthew 26:41*** *"Watch and pray, that ye enter not into temptation: the spirit indeed is willing, but the flash is weak."*
>
> ***Luke 4:13*** *And when the devil had ended all the temptation, he departed from him for a season.*

When Satan appeared to Eve in the garden, he did not tempt her with her desires. He tempted her with doubt of her beliefs. He challenged her beliefs and she failed to live up to what she trusted in, as did Adam. He trusted the woman more than he trusted God.

What is your yoke? We all have a sinful nature, but what about your individual…

Weaknesses?

_____

_____

_____

_____

Temptations?

_____

_____

_____

_____

2. What are you a slave to? A slave is a person that is controlled and owned by another person or thing. The biggest role that plays between person to person is the opinion one holds over another. The desperate need for approval, to control how others think about us, the label one placed on us that we are constantly trying to prove as wrong or to overcome. The insecurity we feel from others who place their opinions and thoughts above all others. This is a constant battle all of us struggle with to overcome or become trapped in. Another slave situation we may feel stuck in is our health. There is nothing like a big dose of chronic illness or pain, or an unexplained illness that's on-going, to leave us exhausted and feeling trapped. It's something we cannot avoid or get away from. It's like a little cloud over our head that follows us everywhere we go and affects the things we try to do or can't do. We feel alone because those around us don't have the experience or understanding of what you face every day and get tired of hearing about it. Some people even withdraw from you and become distant. On some occasions you doubt your illness and people tell you it's all in your head. It controls your activity level, you're eating, you're going out, your relationships, your work, and your play. What about time? You being a slave to the clock. The overwhelming feeling when you just got to work and you feel as though five hours have gone by and you look up at the clock just to realize it's only been 30 minutes. You feel as though this day will never end. The time you spend in misery or unhappiness never seems to end. Or on the other hand, the opportunity of enjoyment never seems to last long enough. You sit back and crave those moments of peace and contentment. You spend all your spare time thinking and preparing for the moment or the weekend when you will enjoy life. When your worst days come, you look for the moment you can just lay your head down on the pillow and pray for sleep to overcome so you can have a break from the misery. Or, you spend so much time chasing the clock of life. If I can do this, I can live longer or be more prosperous. You try your hardest to avoid dying so much that it consumes you. You have children, a spouse, family, grandchildren, friends, and coworkers. They are all depending on you and you must do whatever it takes to live as long as you can for them. Like this is something under your complete control. Control your illness, control your symptoms, control others thoughts, control your time. Sound familiar? These are all issues that we cannot avoid. We become a slave to them because they are part of our lives that we cannot cut out, but we spend so much time trying to avoid or control them. We will even go to lengths of making a rash decision in a hurry to get the quickest relief. To beat time at its own game and we end up worse than when we started. That's leads us to the next questions…

> **_Psalms 90:12_** *So teach [us] to number our days, that we may apply [our] hearts unto wisdom.*

> **_Ecclesiastes 3:1_** *To everything there is a season, and a time to every purpose under the heaven.*

What about triggers? What we often forget or can't get away from is our triggers. For those who don't understand, triggers are thoughts, scenarios, actions, words, smells, phrases, and/or voices that trigger something in our bodies to react in a state of panic, fear, anxiety, doubt, worry, shame, guilt, and/or blame. It is a subconscious automatic response. Some of us have lived within scenarios for long periods of time that put our bodies on automatic. We just automatically react, adjust, and respond to the environment around us. We call this survival mode. The hard part is when we enter into a safe place, our bodies continue to respond to survival mode. The confusion of not knowing how to react within safe perimeters also plagues us. Our fight and flight response have been triggered so much, or the chemical imbalance in our bodies is permanent it becomes part of our everyday lives. It never goes away; it just comes in waves. This scenario makes it very hard for those around us to not understand, so let's paint another picture.

There are two soldiers just came home from war. One soldier lost a leg in combat. It is a physical ailment you can see and sympathize with. Your heart reaches out to him, because you can physically see the impact it has on his life, his movement, his abilities to cope, and the limitations. Your heart goes out to him and you can respect the struggle he faced and went through to get to this point. When he hears gunfire or loud noises, he flinches and reacts and it is completely understandable. The noise is a trigger that sets his body into automatic motion of protection and survival because that is what he is used to doing on a moment by moment basis. Never letting your guard down and always alert. Yet the other one comes home without a scratch to his body, but a gash to his mind. You cannot see the physical ailment on his person, and you don't understand what is wrong with him, why he acts distant. His body is intact and you think he should act grateful,

and my mental cup was almost empty. I was so consumed with my spiritual walk that I totally disregarded all other aspects of life. I had the belief that if I just concentrate spiritually then everything will fall into place. The truth is concentrating on spirituality is just one part of our whole selves needing attention. Let's describe each aspect:

> Spiritual Body: Your beliefs and value system, character, and using your gifts and talents (Notice mental body and spiritual body are two different things, not an indication or factor. They are intertwined, therefore your spiritual life is not up to par. It's about balance and individual growth.).

> Mental Body: Your gaining of knowledge and challenging yourself mentally, mental growth, setting goals, and following through with them, social activity, growth in relationships and friendships.

> Emotional Body: Allowing ourselves to feel, express, accept, and coexist with all our emotions, dealing with past, present, and future emotions.

> Physical Body: Exercise, relaxation, sleep, diet, body of organs, and multiple functions.

Notice here that spiritual, mental, emotional, and physical health body are all separate, yet they have an effect on each other. Each body requires equal attention for the others to function properly. We often look at the body that gives us the most issues and often fail to realize the relief may need to be the balance of another body. Finding out what your values and beliefs are gives you confidence in yourself. Talents and gifts help you know what you are accomplished at and what gives you joy and feelings of accomplishment. Social activities give you a sense of worth and belonging. Emotional expressions help you explore all our emotions we are born having, with experience comes knowledge and understanding of them. Physical exercise, relaxation, sleep, and diet all play a role in how the body handles stress, chemical imbalance, boosting of neurons that are helpful in balancing mood and drive, sleep to reset the brain from day to day, and eating food that is healthy and at regular intervals (especially if you're one of those who gets Hangry!). The hard part is that it requires time. Time that we do not have or time away from something we would rather be doing.

> **_Proverbs 11:1_** *A false <u>balance</u> (scales as a pair, weigh, test, prove consider, to ponder) is an abomination to the LORD, but a just <u>weight</u> (to build, begin to build, repair, obtain children, make, repair, set up) is His delight.*

> **_Deuteronomy 25:13-16_** *Thou shalt not have in thy bag <u>diver's weights</u> (to build), a great and a small. Thou shalt not have in thine house <u>diver's measures</u>, (a receptacle for measuring) a great and a small. But thou shalt have a <u>perfect</u> (complete, peaceable) and <u>just</u> (clear self, to be just) weight, a <u>perfect</u> (complete, peaceable) and <u>just</u> (clear self, to be just) measure shalt thou have: that thy days may be lengthened in the land which the LORD thy God giveth thee. For all that do such things, and all that do <u>unrighteously</u> (to deviate from, to act darkly), are an abomination unto the LORD thy God*

You probably already have a good idea of what is out of balance. Most importantly is for you to see and believe the benefit in finding balance. If you spend every waking moment concentrating on your misery, it will consume you and happiness will be hard to reach.

Try this checklist at http://www.mkprojects.com/checklists-for-health and see if this may help you see what may be out of balance. This list also gives you some tips and ideas to help: https://chopra.com/articles/daily-practices-for-spiritual-mental-emotional-and-physical-well-being#sm.00001nytincdmlemiqv58 uo1htpoa

4. What troublesome laws or expectations do you have on your shoulders that are keeping you from moving forward? These could be expectations you have for yourself or others have for you. The trap of being stuck in an expectation can be so overwhelming. The constant pressure to perform. To be someone you are not or to act as though nothing is ever wrong. I think one of the biggest laws we burden ourselves with as Christians is to be perfect. The expectations to be perfect, act perfect, look perfect, talk perfect. If that is not pressure then I don't know what is.

Or it could be an expectation from your loved ones. I know as a mother, a wife, a woman, there is an overwhelming pressure to be in the kitchen, take care of the kids, do the laundry, grocery shopping, attend every sporting event, keep the house clean at all times, keep the flower beds beautiful, discipline the children correctly, work if necessary, and be ready to make love to your husband at the drop of a hat, regardless of what is going on around you, and to read his mind at all times; to be everyone's emotional support. The father, a husband, a man has the overwhelming expectation of being the money maker (and make more money than his spouse), mow the lawn, trim the bushes, take care of all the vehicles running and maintained, to make all the important decisions for his family and in charge of their well-being at all times, make time for his wife whenever she begins to feel as though she is being ignored, to read her mind at all times, and to be in charge of everyone's spiritual growth.

Then comes the responsibility of being a son or daughter. As your parents get older, they will need more help and care and it will take your time, energy, money, and family to help. To leave your family at an instant and take care of the parents who raised and took care of you. Or on the other hand you have parents that are still dictating to you what your beliefs and values should be. The expectation to live as they want you to live without regard of your own need to work through life and learn from it so you can grow. They still have the overwhelming desire to protect you at all cost or even place their happiness on your shoulders. They continue to blame, shame, or neglect you. Or they are alcoholics or drug addicts stuck in a pattern and only come around when they want or need something and destroy your peace when they do. Or you're the alcoholic or drug addict spending your days trying to avoid the pain of expectations from your own children. A burden of being the perfect parent. You are so overwhelmed with the expectation you want to escape. To run! Maybe you did and the blame and shame of it overwhelms you.

Friends. Some friends accept you as you are and take equal responsibility in the relationship. Others get mad if you don't answer their every phone call. Dependent on you to drop everything at the drop of a hat. Your family, church, and other relationships must not interfere with theirs. They get mad at you for not being the constant emotional support they need. They talk constantly of themselves wanting advice, talking of their struggles and their issues, but when you try to talk with them, they quickly dismiss you, change the subject, or got to go do something else more important. If you don't talk to them every day you are not being a good friend and they will easily discard you as though there is something wrong with you and move on to another friend. Or you may be one of those who have moved around so much in childhood making friends was nearly impossible. You don't really have anyone to confide in, or run things by, or vent to, and you feel alone.

What about the laws and expectations you put on yourself? You pressure yourself to be normal, to act as if nothing has ever affected you. You feel shame and guilt and blame for being the person you are. Others don't accept you for who are and so you are constantly trying to make yourself fit into a mold that is impossible. You are square and have scenarios and struggles that make you have four pointy corners and you try your hardest to fit in the same mold as all those circles who haven't had the experiences you have. The guilt from judgement and condemnation from others leaves you in turmoil because you are not a circle. You don't fit in and you never will so the energy it takes you to keep trying is better spent elsewhere. Or so you think!

> **_Psalms 62:5_** - *My soul, wait thou only upon God; for my expectation [is] from him*
>
> **_Job 8:15_** *He shall lean upon his house, but it shall not stand: he shall hold it fast, but it shall not endure.*
>
> **_Job 15:31_** *Let not him that is <u>deceived</u> (lead astray) trust in <u>vanity</u> (desolating, ruin): for vanity shall be his <u>recompence</u> (compensation).*

What are your expectations or laws that put pressure on you?

Laws or expectations:

_____

_____

_____

_____

Thought or belief about that law or expectation:

_____

_____

_____

_____

With all of these yokes, slavery, balance, and expectation how does one be free? What does the Bible say about being free and gaining freedom with Christ?

<u>Music</u>

("Come to Me" by Kari Jobe)
("Lord I Hope This Day Is Good" by Lauren Duski)

Bringing it All Together

__Matthew 6:24__ No man can serve two masters: for either he will hate the one, and love the other; or else he will hold to the one, and despise the other. Ye cannot serve God and mammon.

With the knowledge we have gained on the yoke, the masters, the work field, and the origin of it all, let's take a look at how they work together as a unit in our daily lives.

Ability of the yoke	Satan as master	God as master
The yoke was used to work animals to help in the assistance of planting and harvesting.	Satan plants thoughts of despair, hopelessness, and doubt, and harvests a life of fear, shame, and guilt.	God plants thoughts of purpose, wholeness, and confidence, and harvests hope, joy, and peace. Jeremiah 29:11
The yoke around the neck and shoulders allows the animal to use their whole strength when pulling. Just placing a yoke around the hips does not allow the animal to use its full capability. The yoke allowed each animal to use 50% more of its power to a task in a given time period.	Satan's goal is for us to be self-reliant, self-power, alone, and depend solely on yourself for everything, including blame for being in the state you are in. Leaving you without full power and ability with the help of others. His help is no help. His power comes from our unbelief in God.	I can do all things through Christ, Philippians 4:13. Gives access to the power of God that can do all things. Seek and ask and it shall be given according to His will, because He has access to the big picture. So, when no answers are there, we can fully trust in Him to take care of it. No action required but to trust. His power comes from our belief in Him.

Yoke is circular in shape, not flexible, and conforms to the shape of the animal, different yokes for different animals.	Temptations are specifically designed based on our genetic makeup, weaknesses, and past experience. Satan is the leader of temptations and they would not exist without him. Satan wants us lost and floundering with who we are and take on blame, shame and guilt instead of embracing who we are.	God is like a circle; He has no beginning and no end. He always was and always will be. Rev 1:8. As our faith and knowledge increase so does the circle of God in our lives increase John 14:6. We our subjected to temptations because of our birth into sin, but with the dying of his son has provided a way out of our sinful state and wiped us clean, John 3:15-16, but also gave us a way to escape the daily temptations that plague us. 1 Corinthians 10:13. He wants us to acknowledge who we are without Him and who we can be with Him and love ourselves as He made us to be.
The use of yoked animals boosted economy and reduced the reliance on sustenance farming.	Rely on power and money to get you through. This provides you with financial stability and takes your focus away from the real issues of emotional stability. More money = more work = no play= no balance = no growth. Or More education = more worthy = more acceptance from others = false sense of worth, etc.	He will supply all your needs. Philippians 4:19 He provided us with the Bible as direction, of medicine to help, and doctors with the gift of dealing with the mind. We are not alone and can call out for help anytime, anywhere.
The use of yoked animals made them more valuable.	Your constant action is required. Must prove your worth at all times, with word, good deeds, being acceptable to everyone.	With God you are whole, enough, complete without need for constant action. He is your portion. Lam 3:24
The use of yoked animals gave people more free time to rest and enjoy their families.	Satan wants you to balance your time on unnecessary things, like TV, sleep, phone, mind wandering, and fantasy to distract you and give you false enjoyment and addiction. Your happiness depends on these things in your life.	God gives you a book of guidance, the open communication to prayer, the ability to help others, and the joy of taking time for yourself. A way to keep your mind focused on what is important to you and your beliefs, which gives you true happiness. Romans 10:17, James 4:8.

The yoke holds you in place with direction from a master.	Satan requires everything you hold dear in order to serve him. It comes with a cost you can't pay.	God requires acceptance, repentance, and reliance. It comes with a cost you can pay. Ephesians 2:8-9
The yoke is designed to run in pairs, it takes two. Two animals or two reins.	Satan as your helper will either stand still and let you do all the work, or will walk backwards to keep you from moving forward. All the while making you think you have done something wrong to be given this burden and that you must pay a cost.	God will not only work beside you and help you carry the load, but when the load gets unbearable, He will pick you up and carry all the load while comforting you in the process and expect nothing in return. Hebrews 13:5

My favorite part is how all that we have studied comes together in a beautiful story of understanding. We have studied the yoke of bondage, using the yoke as an example and the animals as us being directed by a master plowing the brain with our beliefs and values. The yoke is our burden of a sinful nature we are born to that gave us the knowledge of both light and dark. The masters of the light and dark as God and Satan push, driving us to a place of peace or chaos. The mind is our work field. The daily planting of our beliefs by living it until they become deep plowed furrows in our mind. Building up our confidence and dimming all the dark and dreary thoughts that our childhood, trauma, and genetic disposition have left us with. But what is the purpose, the benefit of any of this. As a whole we see this picture as our life, our daily struggle. How do we accept this? How do we adjust to this? How do we have hope in all of this? Is there any freedom?

Music

("King of The World" by Natalie Grant)
("In the Eye of The Storm" by Ryan Stevenson)
("Bless the Broken Road" by Rascal Flatts)

Freedom with the Light

Matthew 11:28-30 *Come unto me, all ye that labour and are heavy laden, and I will give you rest. Take my yoke upon you, and learn of me; for I am meek and lowly in heart: and ye shall find rest unto your souls. For my yoke is easy, and my burden is light.*

Isaiah 10:27 *And it shall come to pass in that day, that his burden shall be taken away from off thy shoulder, and his yoke from off thy neck, and the yoke shall be destroyed because of the anointing"*

Matthew 6:25-34 *Therefore I say unto you, take no thought for your life, what ye shall eat, or what ye shall drink; nor yet for your body, what ye shall put on. Is not the life more than meat, and the body than raiment? Behold the fowls of the air: for they sow not, neither do they reap, nor gather into barns; yet your heavenly Father feedeth them. Are ye not much better than they? Which of you by taking thought can add one cubit unto his stature? And why take ye thought for raiment? Consider the lilies of the field, how they grow; they toil not, neither do they spin: And yet I say unto you, that even Solomon in all his glory was not arrayed like one of these. Wherefore, if God so clothe the grass of the field, which today is, and tomorrow is cast into the oven, shall he not much more clothe you, O ye of little faith? Therefore take no thought, saying, what shall we eat? or, what shall we drink? or, Wherewithal shall we be clothed? (For after all these things do the Gentiles seek:)*

for your heavenly Father knoweth that ye have need of all these things. But seek ye first the kingdom of God, and his righteousness; and all these things shall be added unto you. Take therefore no thought for the morrow: for the morrow shall take thought for the things of itself. Sufficient unto the day is the evil thereof.

So, buckle up, get into a comfy spot where there are no distractions and let the freedom come to you.

1. Read your Bible and work out your own beliefs and values.

Philippians 2:12 *Wherefore, my beloved, as ye have always obeyed, not as in my presence only, but now much more in my absence, work out your own salvation with fear and trembling.*

Romans 8:38-39 *For I am convinced that neither death nor life, neither angels nor demons, neither the present nor the future, nor any powers, neither height nor depth, nor anything else in all creation, will be able to separate us from the love of God that is in Christ Jesus our Lord.*

"Take my yoke upon you, and learn from me, for I am meek and lowly in heart." This is the first step towards freedom is learning from Christ. Not from the preacher, not from your parents, not from your spouse, not from your friends, not from the guy preaching on the radio or TV, but from God! This requires you opening your Bible and reading and studying it. Your yoke from the Lord is to learn and gain knowledge from reading his word. The fact that you have read this all to this point shows you are willing to learn and increase your knowledge. What you will find is a meek and lowly Lord. Not a Lord of demands and large expectations as you find in the world around you, but a Lord that loves you just as you are faults and all.

The hardest part with this is we all have been raised with parents who have their own beliefs and values. To some degree we take on these beliefs and values, yet there are conflicts within it. The reason why is because our life experiences are all different. We will find as we experience things in life not all beliefs and values will line up with every scenario. This is a clear indication it may not be the belief and value the Lord wants you to hold on to. I want nothing more than to be in God's will and know what He values and what are His truths. I want to live a life that measures up. As I have stated before, I have been influenced by verses and scripture misquoted or used for contradictory purposes. This has left me confused and broken because the beliefs I thought where from God did not measure up and I was stuck in a tornado of living right and wrong. It is not about living right or wrong; it's about living with God or without Him. You are either living in the light or living in the dark.

*Living in the light means you have hope within your life no matter what issues, problems, complications, struggles, and temptations assail you. It is a journey of growth and development and ultimate trust and surrender in God. With a promise from Him to make all things turn for the <u>good</u> (benefit). Your heart is of most value and only God has the ability to judge and condemn it for He is the only one who can really see it. No pressure to be in control, but to let God be in control and let everything fall where it may regardless of outcome. Trust time will tell all truths and give God opportunities to work. Where good and bad mean to live for value not for appearance. Fair, honest, or worthy. Living in the Spirit.

*Living in the dark means you are without hope. You are defined by your issues, problems, complications, struggles, and temptations that assail you. You have only yourself to depend on and it's your sole responsibility to keep it together. It is not a journey, but instead a destination of perfection. Your stature is of most importance and everyone has an opinion or value on how you should present yourself and do it. Pressure to be in control, to avoid fear, miscommunications, and hurt feelings. Time is an enemy and allows bad things to take root and grow. A list of good and bad and should and should nots control your daily life, condemnation, selfishness, and pride living in the flesh.

Your beliefs should be constantly growing and changing with knowledge, not stuck in the same pattern. Life is a journey of growth. What you value will become different as you grow and more evident of what it most important to you. If you are stuck, you are not growing. If you are holding on to one specific belief for ages of time and it does not develop into peace, harmony, and edification of others then you are not growing. You are in the dark.

Also, your talents and gifts. God gave each one of us talents and/or spiritual gifts. How are you using them? Are you using them at all? If you do not know your spiritual gifts, try this link and take the test. https://spiritualgiftstest.com/spiritual-gifts-test-adult-version/ What are your talents? Do you even know? Try things out and see what you're drawn to. Build some things, sing, draw, cook, decorate, plan, organize, clean, sew, craft, play games. All of these things are healthy ways to explore what makes you the best you. So, go try and do them.

Take the time to write down what you believe in. What are your talents and gifts?

_____

_____

_____

_____

_____

_____

_____

_____

_____

_____

If you are struggling, try this website and use questionnaire at the bottom. https://www.mindtools.com/pages/article/newTED_85.htm

Checkout the chapter, "What do you believe in?" for a list of questions that might help you. It also includes my own personal answers.

Music

("Flawless" by Mercy Me)
("Road Less Traveled" by Lauren Alaina)
("Hanging On" by Britt Nicole)

2. Think on these things…

__Philippians 4:4-13__ Rejoice in the Lord always: and again I say, Rejoice. Let your moderation be known unto all men. The Lord is at hand. Be careful for nothing; but in every thing by prayer and supplication with thanksgiving let your requests be made known unto God. And the peace of God, which passeth all understanding, shall keep your hearts and minds through Christ Jesus. Finally, brethren, whatsoever things are true, whatsoever things are honest, whatsoever things are just, whatsoever things are pure, whatsoever things are lovely, whatsoever things are of good report; if there be any virtue, and if there be any praise, think on these things. Those things, which ye have both learned, and received, and heard, and seen in me, do: and the God of peace shall be with you. But I rejoiced in the Lord greatly, that now at the last your care of me hath flourished again; wherein ye were also careful, but ye lacked opportunity. Not that I speak in respect of want: for I have learned, in whatsoever state I am, therewith to be content. I know both how to be abased, and I know how to abound: every where and in all things I am instructed both to be full and to be hungry, both to abound and to suffer need. I can do all things through Christ which strengtheneth me.

__2 Corinthians 10:3-5__ For though we walk in the flesh, we do not war after the flesh: (For the weapons of our warfare are not carnal, but mighty through God to the pulling down of strong holds;) Casting down imaginations, and every high thing that exalteth itself against the knowledge of God, and bringing into captivity every thought to the obedience of Christ;

Train of thought…who knew how important our train of thought could play within our peace, contentment, and happiness, let alone in our faith, trust, and confidence. One thing to understand is reining in your train of thought is not an overnight fix. We have years and years of experience letting our minds wander to whatever thought, subject, expectation, want, desire, struggle, fear, shame, blame, and insecurity we can imagine. What we don't realize is the power it can have over our attitude, mood, peace, relationships, and contentment. I think the song by Josh Turner "Long Black Train" gives an excellent picture of our train of thoughts. "Watch out brother for that Long Black Train…look to the heavens and look to the sky…cling to the Father and His Holy name and don't go riding that Long Black Train…. There is an engine on that long black train making you wonder if the ride is worth the pain, He's just waiting for your heart to say, 'Let me ride on that long black train…' I can hear the whistle from a mile away, it sounds so good but I must stay away, that train is a beauty making everybody stare, but its only destination is the middle of nowhere…The

Devil's a driving that long black train". Just because your thoughts feel good and give you temporarily relief, remember they are only a temporary fix that will lead you into a constant circle of nowhere. That's where the devil wants you to be. If you are distracted with a temporary fix then you are distracted from moving forward. What thoughts do you have that often plague you? Or, what thoughts do you have to give you peace and contentment? Are they of the light or of the dark? Do they lead to a solution or to a temporary fix? Are you constantly thinking about what others think? What others should or should not be doing? Is there balance in your thoughts or are they consumed in one area?

The Bible says to think on things that are true, honest, just, pure, lovely, and good report? The best way to know if your thoughts line up with the light is to ask yourself: Is this thought:

Is it true, not concealing, secret, unaware, or without knowing?

Is it honest, honorable, to worship or adore?

Is it just, equitable in character or act, innocent?

Is it pure, modest, clean?

Is it lovely, friendly towards?

Is it of good report, well spoken, reputable?

Yes! All of our minds wander, but are you jumping on that train every time it comes by or are you watching it go by, acknowledging it went by, and in seeing it go by you stay in the moment? Or, are you one of those who will get on the train without knowing it because it has become your norm? I, on the other hand, will get on that train and when I realize I am on it, I scold myself and place blame and shame and guilt for not noticing it sooner, then become anxious because I know I will do it again and try my hardest to avoid it.

Real peace comes by acceptance of the train, know it is there and which thoughts lead to dark places, and those thoughts that lead to the light. Once you realize you are on the train, calmly shift your focus back to the present and smile at yourself for noticing it. Staying in the moment, enjoying the conversations, the people, the relationships you have in front of you. Truly listening to others and taking in what makes them happy or sad, their likes and dislikes, their needs and their wants. Overthinking each scenario before you get there, or predicting every conversation, or judging it keeps you in your head. Stop trying to control it all and just enjoy. Stop judging what is right and wrong and just let the light shine. Bring a smile, a thoughtful word, a listening ear, and a grateful heart. When you are by yourself and the train of thought is so much harder to regulate, just concentrate on what you are doing. If you're eating, eat; If you're watching TV, watch it; if you're washing dishes, wash them; if you're working, work. Don't be thinking about what comes next or what you need to do tomorrow. Stay in the moment. Even if it is something you don't enjoy, allow yourself to acknowledge you don't like it and self-talk yourself into getting through it and finish without avoidance. You will begin to notice that the present you live in is the most true, honest, just, pure, lovely, and of good report that you can focus your mind upon. You will also notice it will become easier and easier to move your mind back to the present the more you try it. It eventually becomes your norm. Living for today. Living in the present no matter what comes your way! What about doing for others? There is no truer, selfless thing to think on than what you can do to help others. The feeling of joy, accomplishment, love. Not overdoing for others, but a balance of doing for others and doing for yourself. If you don't take care of yourself also, you will not be able to help others.

What things are:

True _____

Honest _____

Just _____

Pure _____

Lovely _____

Good Report _____

Ideas you might consider: In the moment thinking, what you are doing right now, meditation, hymns of promise, verses of promise and hope, doing things for others, prayer, conversations with others and truly listening to who they are, what they like, what they don't like, reading, watching an inspired truthful movie, watching Animal Planet or the Discovery Channel, learning something new, a new project, new book, take an art class, take any class, activities such as meditation, mindfulness, interpersonal effectiveness, distress tolerance, and emotional regulation.

Dark thoughts and distractions: What if, catastrophizing, polarizing (black and white), should and should nots, jumping to conclusions, overgeneralizing, filtering, personalization, fallacy of fairness, control fallacies, blaming, global labeling, fallacy of change, emotional reasoning, always being right, heaven's fallacy reward.

3. Accept the Balance of Life...Accept the Yoke

Ecclesiastes 3:1-12

To every thing there is a season, and a time
to every purpose under the heaven:
A time to be born, And a time to die;
A time to plant And at time to pluck up that which is planted;
A time to kill, And a time to heal;
A time to break down, And a time to build up.
A time to weep, And a time laugh;
A time to mourn, And a time to dance;
A time to cast away stones, And a time to gather stones together;
A time to embrace, And a time to refrain from embracing;
A time to get, And a time to lose;
A time to keep, And a time to cast away;
A time to rend, And a time to sew;
A time to keep silence, And a time to speak;
A time to love, And a time to hate;
A time of war, And a time for peace.

__1 Peter 4:1-2__ For as much then as Christ hath suffered
for us in the flesh, arm yourselves likewise with the same
mind: for he that hath suffered in the flesh hath ceased
from sin; That he no longer should live the rest of his time
in the flesh to the lusts of men, but to the will of God.

__Philippians 4:11-13__ Not that I speak in respect of want:
for I have learned, in whatsoever state I am, therewith to be
content. I know both how to be abased, and I know how to
abound: every where and in all things I am instructed both to

> *be full and to be hungry, both to abound and to suffer need.*
> *I can do all things through Christ which strengtheneth me.*

As human beings we spend so much time trying to avoid anything unpleasant from happening. We rush head first into a decision thinking we are doing what is best because it feels right or we fear "what if". The truth of God's message here is to let the time fall where it must and embrace each scenario, also known as acceptance and contentment. It is not about never facing anything hard or uneasy. It's about learning to cope in all types of scenarios and being confident it will all make you more courageous, strong, faithful, and trusting in God's plan for you. God wants you to thrive in all situations and this is not possible if we try to avoid them. Have you ever spent a whole week working and pushing to get through the week and when the weekend came or a day off your joy was overwhelming? By experiencing the work and hard time of pushing through it made the day off so much sweeter! Those who sit on the couch day after day doing everything, they desire to do won't find moments as sweet as this. Why? Because they lack the experience of the struggle. Lack of struggle deflates our moments of joy. There is a time and purpose under heaven, and if you trust and open up your mind to that, the possibilities are endless. This can also pertain to relationships. The relationship that never fights, or argues, or has differences doesn't seem to grow. It becomes stagnant and unfulfilling. But the relationship that takes time, effort, fights, arguments, compromise, or accepts and respects has the ability to grow stronger and stronger with each obstacle or scenario. Trust begins to form and confidence in what you have begins to grow. If you spend your time trying to control this or avoid conflict or not allow time for your relationships to go through the natural flow of things then it will not grow. Ultimately, trusting there is a purpose under heaven for everything we experience and trusting God has a purpose for it.

Another acceptance you have in your life in the acceptance of the state you are in. <u>Accepting</u> (being content with) your mental health issues and/or diagnosis and learning how to cope with it in a healthy way. Mental Illness is not a sign of demonic presence within a person, but through mental illness Satan has a channel to use and attack that person personally and on a very deep and intimate level. Acceptance and acknowledgement of this gives you the ability to find peace in your fate and give hope to an expected end. Or maybe, accepting your loved one has a true illness can lead to a supportive relationship which will grow and become strong. Words of support, encouragement, and love, not blame and shame. Blame and shame are usually followed with a list of things you should be doing and these are not words of acceptance. Try to have patience with your loved one instead of constantly being ill with them because of their struggle. When you are in a state of acceptance, it can help your loved one who is struggling to get there also! If you cannot get to acceptance then acknowledge it and give your loved one space with others who can!

Accept the hurt! Faith in God does not get rid of the hurt, but neither does drowning yourself with alcohol or pills or food or caffeine or nicotine. It may give you some temporary relief, but the effects of the hurt will still remain. The hurt others have done to you, the hurt of your current condition, the hurt of failure, the hurt of being misunderstood, the hurt of lost loved ones, the hurt of abuse, all of these have pain that come with them. Sometimes this pain can be physical. Sometimes it is emotional. A lot of times it is both. The biggest part of acceptance is not trying to avoid the hurt, but to work through it. To face the fear the hurt brings with it. The sorrow, the guilt, the shame, the blame, the damage, the life you wish you had but don't kind of hurt. Somewhere in the acceptance of this you can find freedom. Freedom to let that hurt enter into your life and try to make something beautiful with it. Accept you may not measure up in the eyes of others and never will, but that in God's eyes you do! To give us hope! Some call it a change in attitude, but another word for attitude is perspective. With Gods help, pray and ask for a change is perspective. Ask him to show you the possibilities. When we are so overwhelmed with fear and hopelessness, we need help switching gears in our minds.

> **Romans 8:18** *For I reckon that the sufferings of this present time [are] not worthy [to be compared] with the glory which shall be revealed in us.*

> **Revelation 21:4** *And God shall wipe away all tears from their eyes; and there shall be no more death, neither sorrow, nor crying, neither shall there be any more pain: for the former things are passed away.*

> **Psalms 147:3** *He healeth the broken in heart, and bindeth up their wounds.*

Accept God has brought me down this path or will leave me on this path for the strengthening of my faith, so I may keep it and grow strong in it. Not for the purpose of punishment for lack of faith, but the purpose of proving, deciding, and refining my beliefs. Trusting He has a purpose for it all!

> **1 Peter 4:11-19** *Beloved, think it not strange concerning the fiery trial which is to try you, as though some strange thing happened unto you: But rejoice,*

inasmuch as ye are partakers of Christ's sufferings; that, when his glory shall be revealed, ye may be glad also with exceeding joy. If ye be reproached for the name of Christ, happy [are ye]; for the spirit of glory and of God resteth upon you: on their part he is evil spoken of, but on your part he is glorified. But let none of you suffer as a murderer, or [as] a thief, or [as] an evildoer, or as a busybody in other men's matters. Yet if [any man suffer] as a Christian, let him not be ashamed; but let him glorify God on this behalf. For the time [is come] that judgment must begin at the house of God: and if [it] first [begin] at us, what shall the end [be] of them that obey not the gospel of God? And if the righteous scarcely be saved, where shall the ungodly and the sinner appear? Wherefore let them that suffer according to the will of God commit the keeping of their souls [to him] in well doing, as unto a faithful Creator.

1 Peter 5:10 *But the God of all grace who hath called us unto his eternal glory by Christ Jesus, after that ye have suffered a while, make you perfect, stablish, strengthen, settle you.*

What things do you find difficult to accept or be content with? What small steps can you make in the direction of learning to accept these things and be content?

Difficult Things	Steps

Music

("Even If" by Mercy Me)
("Thy Will" by Hillary Scott)
("It Is Well with My Soul" by Carrie Underwood)
("Let It Go" by Demi Lovato)
("Malibu" by Miley Cyrus)
("Stand in The Light" by Jordan Smith)

4. Time...What are you doing with your time, what are you thinking about when you do it?

Ecclesiastes 3:13 What profit hath he that worketh in that wherin he laboureth? I have seen the travail (to bear) which God hath given to the sons of men to be exercised in it. He hath made everything beautiful in his time. Also he hath set the world in their heart, so that no man can find out the work that God maketh from the beginning to the end. I know that there is no good in them, but for a man to rejoice, and to do good in his life. And also that every man should eat and drink, and enjoy the good of all his labour, it is the gift of God.

Proverbs 16:11 A just(verdict) weight (balance, scale) and balance (scales, test, prove, consider) are the LORD's: all the weights of the bag are his work.

Leviticus 19:35-36 Ye shall do no unrighteousness in judgment, in meteyard, in weight, or in measure. Just balances, just weights, a just ephah, and a just hin, shall ye have: I am the LORD your God, which brought you out of the land of Egypt

---

Is there a balance of time in your day? Here we see that balance is of the Lord. A thing of light. A balance of justice for crime, vengeance for wrong doing, peace for the weary, etc. A just weight and balance are the Lord's. The Lord favors balance. Can this not also include the balance of your life and time? Could this not also be a loving reminder for us to seek balance. This is not about control; it's about balance. An equal measure of two or more objects. Finding a balance allows us to explore every aspect of who we are. If we worked all the time then we would be in constant work mode and our bodies would not know how to play. If we are in constant sorrow, we have no joy. If we constantly play, our bodies wouldn't know how to work. If we constantly eat, our bodies would never know when we're truly hungry. If we are always hungry, our bodies would never know the comfort of being full. If we always exercised, our muscles would never relax. If we always relax, our muscles would never grow strong. If our minds are in constant go mode, we won't sleep. If we don't sleep, our minds become anxious. If I always read my Bible then I wouldn't have time to pray and talk to God. If I always prayed then I would not hear God speak to me through His word. I could go on and on, but can you see the importance of balancing our activities and even our thoughts.

Take the time to make sure you have balance. You know exactly what is out of balance, and more than likely you know what you are afraid to do within the balance because your thoughts will come in and steal what joy you have. Practice makes perfect so take 10 min to go for a walk. On that walk don't think about your anxiety or problems. Think about your body. Think about the feeling of the sun on your face, or the wind, or the cold. Think about your breathing. Think about your feet touching the ground. Look at the trees or grass or flowers around you. Can you name any of them? Before long, you will find some peace of not being in your head and enjoying a quiet moment. These things are true, pure, lovely, and of good report. It may be hard at first and you may not want to do it. But continue to push forward and try. Take 10 minutes every day this week, then next week take 12 minutes. It's a process of practice for your mind. Exercise it, give it some rest, give it a break. Be willing to make a change.

Food for thought? The Bible says our body is a temple for the holy spirit. I have constantly heard that because of such we should not defile the body with piercings and tattoos and such, but is that truly what it is saying? Is that your belief or someone else's? But how about the body is the temple and therefore you need to honor it and take care of it. It's not about taking care of your stature or your appearance, but about taking care of the body that is holding the spirit. As we have studied, the spirit is what is of the most value? What are we doing for our bodies to take care of our spirit?

> ***1 Corinthians 6:19*** *What? know ye not that your body is the temple of the Holy Ghost which is in you, which ye have of God, and ye are not your own?*

> ***1 Corinthians 15:44*** *It is sown a natural body; it is raised a spiritual body. There is a natural body, and there is a spiritual body.*

> ***1 Corinthians 15:38-41*** *But some* man *will say, how are the dead raised up? and with what body do they come?* Thou *fool, that which thou sowest is not quickened, except it die: And that which thou sowest, thou sowest not that body that shall be, but bare grain, it may chance of wheat, or of some other* grain*: But God giveth it a body as it hath pleased him, and to every seed his own body. All flesh* is *not the same flesh: but* there is *one* kind *of flesh of men, another flesh of beasts, another of fishes,* and *another of birds.* There are *also celestial bodies, and bodies terrestrial: but the glory of the celestial* is *one, and the* glory *of the terrestrial* is *another.* There is *one glory of the sun, and another glory of the moon, and another glory of the stars: for* one *star differeth from* another *star in glory.*

Things you may need to take time for and balance:
Sleep, exercise, therapy, or time with others venting and

talking, faith- reading, studying, and growing your faith and beliefs, household chores, work, helping others, me time

What do you spend your day doing?

Time	Activity	Hours spent doing that activity
Example: 11:30pm to 7:30am	Sleep	8 hours

What do I spend the most time doing?

What do I spend the least time doing?

Is there an equal balance of mental, physical, emotional, and spiritual time? Try this checklist at http://www.mkprojects.com/checklists-for-health and see if this may help you see what may be out of balance.

Use this list to help you get it back in check: https://chopra.com/articles/daily-practices-for-spiritual-mental-emotional-

and-physical-well-being#sm.00001nytincdmlemiqv58uo1ht
poa

Which one(s) are out of balance?

What am I thinking about when I do these activities?

5. Expectation and Judgement

> ***Psalms 62:5*** *My soul, wait thou only upon
> God; for my expectation is from him.*

> ***Philippians 1:20*** *According to my earnest expectation
> and my hope, that in nothing I shall be ashamed, but that
> with all boldness, as always, so now also Christ shall be
> magnified in my body, whether it be by life, or by death.*

> ***James 4:12*** *There is one lawgiver, who is able to save
> and to destroy: who art thou that judgest another?*

> ***1 Corinthians 4:4*** *For I know nothing by myself; yet am I
> not hereby justified: but he that judgeth me is the Lord.*

> ***1 Corinthians 4:5*** *Therefore judge nothing before the time,
> until the Lord come, who both will bring to light the hidden
> things of darkness, and will make manifest the counsels of
> the hearts: and then shall every man have praise of God.*

A few definitions to understand before we move forward

Word	Bible Definition	Reference
Expectation	Ground for hope	Psalm 62:5, Prov 10:28
Judgement	To distinguish or decided for or against	Romans 5:16
Condemnation	justice, a separating, a tribunal	John 5:24, Romans 5:16
Righteousness	cleansed, made justified, put to rights, It Comes to fullness when we get to heaven	Galatians 5:5, Psalm 33:18-22
Hope	waiting for something we cannot see with confidence, anticipate with pleasure	Isaiah 40:31, Romans 8:25

There are three types of expectations:
Expectations from others,
Expectations from ourselves,
Expectations from God.

As well as three types of Judgement:
Judgement from others,
Judgement from ourselves,
Judgement from God to everyone.

Within the existence of this world I have learned expectation is usually a measure given based on some kind of judgement. For instance, we judge ourselves based on how much money we make, therefore we have an expectation to have an education, job, or career to get a job making as much money as we can. But what we miss is the purpose or reason behind that judgment. Sometimes we overlook the deep meaning behind a judgment and take things at face value. "Well the world looks at it that way, so in order for me to make it in this world I must look at it that way." What we are truly saying is my value and importance are based on how much money I make. For some of us it's not about money instead it may be about how many things you can accomplish in this life, how many toys you can acquire, how many clothes you can acquire, how many friends you have, how many people approve of you, how big of a house you have, how skinny you are, how many church services and functions you attend, how many "successful" children you have, or how many people you can give advice to on a daily basis. What you will also find is you will judge others by this same measure. But are any of these accomplishments a true standard to measurement our worth and value or someone else's worth and value? How does God measure our value?

<u>Understanding Judgement</u>

Understanding judgement takes care of expectation since they go hand in hand. The Bible clearly states, "Judge not, that ye be not judged, for with what judgement ye judge, ye shall be judged and with what measure ye mete, it shall be measured to you again." Matt 7:1 and Luke 6:37. Here we find a great warning of judgement. We are in danger of judgement by the measure of judgement we deliver to others. God also gives us direction on how to correct this behavior, "And as ye would that men should do to you, do also to them likewise." Luke 6:31. Treat others how you want to be treated. The greatest verse we will find on how to treat others is, "A new commandment I give unto you, that ye love one another; as I have loved you, that ye also love one another." John 13:34. Also found in John 13:55, John 15:12, John 15:17,

Romans 12:10, Romans 13:8, Galatians 5:13, Ephesians 4:2, 1 Thessalonians 3:12, 1 Thessalonians 4:9, Hebrews 10:24, 1 Peter 1:22, 1 Peter 3:8, 1 John 3:11, 1 John 3:23, 1 John 4:7, 11,12, and 1 John 1:5. Nineteen verses on loving one another. Notice though, this verse starts out "A New commandment I give to you…" Not only are these words significant, but the location of these verses was all during Jesus' ministry on earth and after his crucifixion. A new way of behavior, a new beginning with his sacrifice, a new way of seeing things. We get so caught up in the tradition of religion. Following a list of rules of dos and don'ts, should and should nots. A list of judgements to measure ourselves and others by as they did before Jesus' coming to earth that we lose sight of the main reason Jesus came to earth. To free us from that!! To free us from the law and move us into grace…Let's define them.

> **_Romans 11:6_** *And if by grace, then is it no more of works: otherwise grace is no more grace. But if it be of works, then it is no more grace: otherwise work is no more work.*

> **_Galatians 2:16_** *Knowing that a man is not justified by the works of the law, but by the faith of Jesus Christ, even we have believed in Jesus Christ, that we might be justified by the faith of Christ, and not by the works of the law: for by the works of the law shall no flesh be justified.*

> **_Galatians 3_** *O foolish Galatians, who hath bewitched you, that ye should not obey the truth, before whose eyes Jesus Christ hath been evidently set forth, crucified among you? This only would I learn of you, Received ye the Spirit by the works of the law, or*

by the hearing of faith? Are ye so foolish? having begun in the Spirit, are ye now made perfect by the flesh? Have ye suffered so many things in vain? if it be yet in vain. He therefore that ministereth to you the Spirit, and worketh miracles among you, doeth he it by the works of the law, or by the hearing of faith? Even as Abraham believed God, and it was accounted to him for righteousness. Know ye therefore that they which are of faith, the same are the children of Abraham. And the scripture, foreseeing that God would justify the heathen through faith, preached before the gospel unto Abraham, saying, in thee shall all nations be blessed. So then they which be of faith are blessed with faithful Abraham. For as many as are of the works of the law are under the curse: for it is written, cursed is every one that continueth not in all things which are written in the book of the law to do them. But that no man is justified by the law in the sight of God, it is evident: for, the just shall live by faith. And the law is not of faith: but, the man that doeth them shall live in them. Christ hath redeemed us from the curse of the law, being made a curse for us: for it is written, cursed is every one that hangeth on a tree. That the blessing of Abraham might come on the Gentiles through Jesus Christ; that we might receive the promise of the Spirit through faith. Brethren, I speak after the manner of men; Though it be but a man's covenant, yet if it be confirmed, no man disannulleth, or addeth thereto. Now to Abraham and his seed were the promises made. He saith not, and to seeds, as of many; but as of one, and to thy seed, which is Christ. And this I say, that the covenant, that was confirmed before *of God in Christ, <u>the law</u>, which was four hundred and thirty years after, cannot disannul, that it should make the promise of none effect. For if the inheritance be of the law, it is no more of promise: but God gave it to Abraham by promise. Wherefore then serveth the law? It was added because of transgressions, till the seed should come to whom the promise was made; and it was ordained by angels in the hand of a mediator. Now a mediator is not a mediator of one, but God is one. Is the law then against the promises of God? God forbid: for if there had been a law given which could have given life, verily righteousness should have been by the law. But the scripture hath concluded all under sin, that the promise by faith of Jesus Christ might be given to them that believe. But before faith came, we were kept under the law, shut up unto the faith which should afterwards be revealed. Wherefore the law was our schoolmaster to bring us unto Christ, that we might be justified by faith. But after that faith is come, we are no longer under a schoolmaster. For ye are all the children of God by faith in Christ Jesus. For as many of you as have been baptized into Christ have put on Christ. There is neither Jew nor Greek, there is neither bond nor free, there is neither male nor female: for ye are all one in Christ Jesus. And if ye be Christ's, then are ye Abraham's seed, and heirs according to the promise.*

<u>Titus 3:5</u> *Not by works of righteousness which we have done, but according to his mercy he saved us, by the washing of regeneration, and renewing of the Holy Ghost;*

<u>Ephesians 2:8-9</u> *For by grace are ye saved through faith; and that not of yourselves: [it is] the gift of God: Not of works, lest any man should boast.*

<u>Romans 3:19-31</u> *Now we know that what things soever the law saith, it saith to them who are under the law: that every mouth may be stopped, and all the world may become guilty before God. Therefore by the deeds of the law there shall no flesh be justified in his sight: for by the law is the knowledge of sin. But now the righteousness of God without the law is manifested, being witnessed by the law and the prophets; Even the righteousness of God which is by faith of Jesus Christ unto all and upon all them that believe: for there is no difference: For all have sinned, and come short of the glory of God; Being justified freely by his grace through the redemption that is in Christ Jesus: Whom God hath set forth to be a propitiation through faith in his blood, to declare his righteousness for the remission of sins that are past, through the forbearance of God; To declare, I say, at this time his righteousness: that he might be just, and the justifier of him which believeth in Jesus. Where is boasting then? It is excluded. By what law? of works? Nay: but by the law of faith. Therefore we conclude that a man is justified by faith without the deeds of the law. Is he the God of the Jews only? is he not also of the Gentiles? Yes, of the Gentiles also: Seeing it is one God, which shall justify the circumcision by faith, and uncircumcision through faith. Do we then make void the law through faith? God forbid: yea, we establish the law.*

Law- A covenant made between God and man before his crucifixion to introduce a way to identify transgressions. A custom, the Old Testament, the <u>works</u> of following a moral set of rules to gain acceptance and salvation. A list of rules to carry out in order to find forgiveness and escape condemnation. Necessary brought before grace in order to pave a way in men's hearts to accept grace.

Grace- A gift, the option to choose the knowledge (have faith) that works are not required to gain acceptance and salvation. It is a free gift, that by the sacrifice Jesus gave of His body (shedding of innocent blood) created a way where only Faith is required to gain salvation. That you are accepted, loved, and adored for who you are and there is an infinity of forgiveness waiting for you with your faith in Him. Followed by a desire to live upright and seek God's help and leadership. While being truthful and honest with God in all things with repentance. Where God sees you as whole, enough, unblemished, beautiful, strong, and courageous. A promise made to us by God.

Law requires work, a work that you can do all on your own. Grace requires faith, faith which transforms into hope. Can you see the difference? Which one do you follow on a daily basis? Which one do you present to others when you look at them, talk with them, treat them? Which one do you live by? Which one do you transfer onto yourself? Better yet, which one do others in your life press upon you? As we move forward from thinking in the way of the law and moving to a thinking of grace, let's give right and wrong and good and bad new definitions. As you read the Bible and study you will find that as grace becomes possible two words are more often used. Instead of right and wrong you will find light and dark. Two words we have also defined as living in dark and living in light. So instead of asking yourself is this right or wrong or should I do this or should I do that? Think, is this from the light or from the dark? Are my reasons coming from a helpful standpoint or fearful one?

God's Judgement

There is no better freedom in knowledge than to know how God judges us. It is absolutely amazing after I study this how free and clear headed I become! Better yet, it also frees me from the judgement of others because it clearly defines how others do not have the ability to judge you. It does not take away the hurt you have from their treatment, but I hope it gives you peace in knowing that God does not see you as the world does.

1 Samuel 16:7 But the Lord said unto Samuel, look not on his countenance, or on the height of his stature; because I have refused him: for the Lord seeth not as man seeth; for man looketh on the outward appearance, but the Lord looketh on the heart.

Proverbs 16:2 *All the ways of a man are clean in his own eyes; but the Lord weigheth the spirits.*

Isaiah 55:8,9 *For my thoughts are not your thoughts, neither are your ways my ways, saith the Lord. For as the heavens are higher than the earth, so are my ways higher than your ways, and my thoughts than your thoughts.*

God does not judge us based on our actions, words, and/or deeds. God looks at our hearts! Our motif for why we do what we do. Because our knowledge of things is so small and each one of us have a different measure of knowledge there is no way one standard works for everyone. You may say, well there are other verses that tell me whether or not someone is a true "Christian or not" like Galatians 5:22, but can you tell if someone is doing those things for appearance or truly from a heart of love and devotion. We can only see what is in front of us, but we do not have the ability to see the motive of why someone is doing what they are. Take for instance a person who is hooked on drugs. All you see is a dirty druggy who lies, steals, cheats, and does everything they can for their next high. God sees a person who is hurting, traumatized, stuck, confused, and struggling. There is always an underlying story that you do not know exists and this does not allow you to judge.

1 Corinthians 6:5 *I speak to your shame. Is it so, that there is not a wise man among you? No, not one* *that shall be able <u>to judge</u> (to separate thoroughly, to withdraw from) between his brethren*

<u>1 Corinthians 10:29-32</u> *Conscience, I say, not thine own, but of the other: for why is my liberty judged (to distinguish to decide mentally or judicially, to implicate in order to try for punishment) of another man's conscience? For if we would judge ourselves, we should not be judged. But when we are judged, we are chastened of the Lord, that we should not be condemned with the world.*

<u>James 4:11-12</u> *Speak not evil one of another, brethren. He that speaketh evil of his brother, and judgeth his brother, speaketh evil of the <u>law</u> (parceling out of regulations, and or justice) and judgeth the law: but if thou judge the law, thou art not a doer of the law, but a judge. There is one lawgiver, who is able to save and to destroy: who art thou that judgest another?*

(Notice Again, we see the use of law in three different ways. We have a book of law, living by the law, and law as in giving of justice)

So, we know that God judges based on the heart, but when does he judge? Does he judge us every day? Are the results of my mental disorder a judgement from God? So, let's define the difference between God's judgement and the world's judgement before we move on so we have a distinction between them, because I really want you to understand God and how he sees you!

World judgement- Judgement in the form of consequences for actions, words, or deeds, we have done or others have done that affect our daily lives. Some consequences are healthy and some are not.

__Galatians 6:7-8__ Be ye not deceived God is not mocked. For whatsoever a man soweth that shall he also reap. For he that soweth to his flesh shall of the flash reap corruption; but he that soweth to the Spirit shall of the Spirit reap life everlasting.

__Job 4:8__ - Even as I have seen, they that plow iniquity, and sow wickedness, reap the same

__Proverbs 26:27__ - Whoso diggeth a pit shall fall therein: and he that rolleth a stone, it will return upon him

God's judgment- Judgement passed to us on our last day at an appointed time.

__John 12:48-__ He that rejecteth me, and receiveth not my words, hath one that judgeth him: the word that I have spoken, the same shall judge him in the last day

__1 Corinthians 4:3-5__ But with me it is a very small thing that I should be judged of you or of man's judgement: yea, I judge not mine own self. For I know nothing by myself; yet am I not hereby justified: but he that judgeth me is the Lord. Therefore, judge nothing before the time, until the Lord come who both will bring light the hidden things of darkness, and will make manifest the counsels of the hearts: and then shall every man have praise of God.

__Psalm 75:2__ When I shall receive the congregation I will judge uprightly.

2 Peter 3:9 - *The Lord is not slack concerning his promise, as some men count slackness; but is longsuffering to us-ward, not willing that any should perish, but that all should come to repentance.*

Jeremiah 17:9-10 The heart [is] deceitful above all [things], and desperately wicked: who can know it? I the LORD search the heart, [I] try the reins, even to give every man according to his ways, [and] according to the fruit of his doings.

Hebrews 9:27 - And as it is appointed unto men once to die, but after this the judgment

God judgeth on the last day, the day when all dark things are not hidden and brought to the light. With judgement God does not judge us on a daily basis and hand out punishment. Why? Because how can God punish us for what we did last week if we are going to repent of it the day before we die? Can there be worldly consequences for our decisions? Yes! But God's ultimate judgement. No! God says "Fear Not" 365 times in the Bible. One for each day of the year. I do not find this as a coincidence, but a revelation of God saying I do not want you as a Christian to live in the fear of judgement for every second of your life. I do not want you to live in a world of expectations you cannot accomplish every day of your life. That is not what I designed you for. That is not your purpose. There have been many times I have heard the phrase: "You better straighten up and live right or God will take you out, or take away your gifts and your talents". I do not believe that God is that kind of God, because there is no love and justice in it. How can God go ahead and judge me and hand out punishments on a daily basis?

<u>Romans 5</u> *Therefore being justified by faith, we have peace with God through our Lord Jesus Christ: By whom also we have access by faith into this grace wherein we stand, and rejoice in hope of the glory of God. And not only so, but we glory in tribulations also: knowing that tribulation worketh patience; And patience, experience; and experience, hope: And hope maketh not ashamed; because the love of God is shed abroad in our hearts by the Holy Ghost which is given unto us. For when we were yet without strength, in due time Christ died for the ungodly. For scarcely for a righteous man will one die: yet peradventure for a good man some would even dare to die. But God commendeth his love toward us, in that, while we were yet sinners, Christ died for us. Much more then, being now justified by his blood, we shall be saved from wrath through him. For if, when we were enemies, we were reconciled to God by the death of his Son, much more, being reconciled, we shall be saved by his life. And not only so, but we also joy in God through our Lord Jesus Christ, by whom we have now received the atonement. Wherefore, as by one man sin entered into the world, and death by sin; and so, death passed upon all men, for that all have sinned: (For until the law sin was in the world: but sin is not imputed when there is no law. Nevertheless, death reigned from Adam to Moses, even over them that had not sinned after the similitude of Adam's transgression, who is the figure of him that was to come. But not as the offence, so also is the free gift. For if through the offence of one many be dead, much more the grace of God, and the gift by grace, which is by one man, Jesus*

Christ, hath abounded unto many. And not as it was by one that sinned, so is the gift: for the judgment was by one to condemnation, but the free gift is of many offences unto justification. For if by one man's offence death reigned by one; much more they which receive abundance of grace and of the gift of righteousness shall reign in life by one, Jesus Christ. Therefore, as by the offence of one judgment came upon all men to condemnation; even so by the righteousness of one the free gift came upon all men unto justification of life. For as by one man's disobedience many were made sinners, so by the obedience of one shall many be made righteous. Moreover, the law entered, that the offence might abound. But where sin abounded, grace did much more abound: That as sin hath reigned unto death, even so might grace reign through righteousness unto eternal life by Jesus Christ our Lord.

This chapter brings chill bumps to my arms. How perfectly drawn out for us. God's judgment, condemnation, and love for us. Faith in God allows us access to peace with God, access to His grace, and access to joy. For we can rejoice in our tribulations for through our tough times we develop patience and it turns into hope. For when we were without strength and weakened from Adam's sins and subjected to a life of separation for God, He sent His son to die for us and by doing this gave us grace. We were in judgement and condemnation (a decree and decision made by a crime, penalty by death) by Adam's sin. Through the shedding of His son's blood we are moved into many offences with justification (unintentional error with a right to render innocent and free), where sin exists, but grace is more abundant. Grace is so much greater than judgement and condemnation. It can lead us to be seen as equitable in character and in act. Grace declares us as innocent and free. WOW!!! Our faith in God, our trust, our hope, leave us without blame, innocent in the eyes of God. If God sees us that way, why can we not look at ourselves that way? Or even others? This paints a clear picture for us on how we need to see ourselves. God sees us as innocent people caught up in the sin of Adam. Born into a sinful nature of knowing good and evil. He sent us a way out of this scenario: by faith! We can either accept the gift of His son and seek to believe and hope in His gracious gift or we can reject it and continue to live in judgement and condemnation.

I won't lie, as a believer in Christ's grace I struggle every day to keep my faith intact. The spiritual battle within me is in constant struggle to keep my head above the water and keep my eyes on Jesus as Peter did. But regardless of how others see me, judge me, tell me how right and wrong I am, I am cleansed clean by the love of God and the gift of His grace and it may take me every day of my life to acknowledge and believe it, but I will do it. Will it come at a price for me? Yes! Because in an imperfect world there is no way to avoid heartache and pain. But I choose to do it with God on my side instead of without him. I choose!! That's right! We all have the right and the freedom to choose! So, what do you choose to believe?

Judging others and what healthy expectations we can have

It is so easy for us to play the Judge and jury for those around us. We can look into their lives without bias and clearly see what the problem is and sufficiently give correction. But can we? What about for ourselves? Can we clearly look into our lives and clearly judge ourselves? The answer would be no! Why is this? Well, because of our lack of knowledge. The only way we can properly judge ourselves and others is if we have a complete knowledge of all things. We don't as we have already studied. Our knowledge is limited with inexperience and ignorance. There is no blame and shame in it. It just is what it is. But how can we be free of that? Well, to concentrate on what we can do, the Lord puts it into perspective in 1 John 3.

In what ways do you experience judgement, what is the expectation that follows, and what do you believe?

Judgement	Expectation	Your Belief

This chart shows us not only what judgements we experience, but most importantly the expectation and belief that fuel the judgement. For me it is easier to start with the belief. For example, I believe that there is great value in how others see me or what they think about me. That others opinions about me are a true reflection of my character. With that comes the expectation to constantly focus on rising above whatever standard others think I don't have. Because let's face it, others opinions of me are never good. That brings me to the category of judgement. The judgement that this person thinks bad about me because of the way she talks to me, looks at me, opens up to me, or talks to others about me. All of this derived from the core belief that others opinions of me should matter.

Are these expectations ridiculous? Yes! Are they biblical? No! For those of us living with mental health issues the struggle makes these core beliefs hard to see. What is amazing here is if you can change your belief, you can change the expectation and the judgement.

For example:

Others opinions do not hold great value and is not a true measure of my worth. No one but God can see me heart (1 Samuel 16:7). No one truly knows everything about me and what I have been through. This also goes for other people. I cannot measure their worth based on any one decision, choice, or event in another person's life. For I truly do not know the whole story.

The expectation changes to just do the best I can do with God helps. Concentrate on how God sees me. Pray. Pray for others and be encouraging and supportive if possible. Pray for myself. Ask for wisdom, strength, and confidence in my beliefs.

Judgement changes to. I am going through a hard time and it does not define me as a person, but is a true reflection of life's never-ending struggles we all face. Or for others we can say, "That person is going through a hard time. They must have something significant going on. They must be struggling. They are not the only ones."

The more we can practice this breakdown, the brain fog clears and the clarity we need comes. We begin to see the core beliefs we have instilled in our hearts without realizing it. How they affect how we treat others and ourselves. Then with the change in belief comes the change in expectations and the freedom God wants us to have in Him.

6. Prayer

Romans 12:12 *Rejoicing in hope; patient in tribulation; continuing instant in prayer;*

Psalms 5:3 *My voice shalt thou hear in the morning, O LORD; in the morning will I direct my prayer unto thee, and will look up*

Matthew 21:22 *And all things, whatsoever ye shall ask in prayer, believing, ye shall receive.*

Luke 6:12 *And it came to pass in those days, that he went out into a mountain to pray, and continued all night in prayer to God.*

Philippians 4:6 *Be careful for nothing; but in everything by prayer and supplication with thanksgiving let your requests be made known unto God.*

James 4:6 *If any of you lack wisdom, let him ask of God, that giveth to all men liberally, and upbraideth not; and it shall be given him. But let him ask in faith, nothing wavering. For he that wavereth is like a wave of the sea driven with the wind and tossed.*

Prayer is our communication line with God. By prayer we make the action of securing our faith, hope, and trust in Him. I could not go on without expressing to you how wonderful prayer is. Prayer lets you be as close to God or as far away from God as you desire. You can seek Him in all things and confide in Him as a friend or you can go to Him in times of need. But what I can tell you is God desires you to talk to Him, ask Him for help, tell Him of your joys, your gratefulness, to experience life with you, to be as one. I will not tell you how easy this is because it is so hard when the conversation seems one-sided. But if you truly are in tune with God and are studying His word with prayer, He will make clear to you in His time all the answers. Whether it's the one you want to hear or not. But most importantly is to believe and trust that whatever happens He is working things for our good. An example I heard from an interview with Janine Turner on "I am Second" never left me. Our lives are one big quilt, all we can see are the threads. The tiny threads and many of them, but God can see the whole quilt, the big picture of our lives. Faith in Him helps us let go of dreading and anticipating what is to come, feeling damaged from our past, and knowing deep in our hearts we are never alone!

> **Deuteronomy 31:8** *And the LORD, he it is that doth go before thee; he will be with thee, he will not fail thee, neither forsake thee: fear not, neither be dismayed.*

> **Psalm 91** My personal favorite scripture!!- *He that dwelleth in the secret place of the Most High shall abide under the shadow of the Almighty. I will say of the LORD, He is my refuge and my fortress: my God; in him will I trust. Surely, he shall deliver thee from the snare of the fowler, and from the noisome pestilence. He shall cover thee with his feathers, and under his wings shalt thou trust: his truth shall be thy shield and buckler. Thou shalt not be afraid for the terror by night; nor for the arrow that flieth by day; Nor for the pestilence that walketh in darkness; nor for the destruction that wasteth at noonday. A thousand shall fall at thy side, and ten thousand at thy right hand; but it shall not come nigh thee. Only with thine eyes shalt thou behold and see the reward of the*

wicked. Because thou hast made the LORD, which is my refuge, even the most High, thy habitation; There shall no evil befall thee, neither shall any plague come nigh thy dwelling. For he shall give his angels charge over thee, to keep thee in all thy ways. They shall bear thee up in their hands, lest thou dash thy foot against a stone. Thou shalt tread upon the lion and adder: the young lion and the dragon shalt thou trample under feet. Because he hath set his love upon me, therefore will I deliver him: I will set him on high, because he hath known my name. He shall call upon me, and I will answer him: I will be with him in trouble; I will deliver him, and honour him. With long life will I satisfy him, and shew him my salvation.

God goes before us and all things go through him before they reach us. Kind of like a buffer. We concentrate on the fact He doesn't keep bad things from happening to us. We get mad as Him. When the truth is God is a fair and just God. God can take all the hurt, pain, and suffering we have and use it to grow us, refine us, and lift us up in our faith. He does all of this while truly being fair at the same time. This is what makes God so good! But the question remains…Are you resting in the shadow of the Almighty? Are you truly praying, asking, and trusting in Him for help, and accepting the answer He gives you, trusting He knows what is best? Are you asking God to help you trust Him for help? He doesn't expect us to do anything on our own!!!! Nothing! This world tells us if we ask for help, seek for help, desire help, then we are weak and to show weakness is not acceptable. But God says:

__James 4:10__ Humble yourselves in the sight of the Lord and He will lift you up.

__1 Peter 5:6__ Humble yourselves therefore under the mighty hand of God, that he may exalt you in due time

__1 Peter 5:5__ Likewise ye younger, submit yourselves unto the elder. Yea, all of you be subject one to another, and be clothed with humility: for God resisteth the proud, and giveth grace to the humble.

__Matthew 23:12 and Luke 14:11__ For whosoever shall exalt himself shall be abased; and he that shall humble himself shall be exalted.

__Matthew 18:4__ Whosoever shall humble himself as this little child, the same is greatest in the kingdom of heaven.

__Philippians 2:8__ And being found in fashion as a man, he humbled himself, and became obedient unto death, even the death of the cross.

To be humble is not weakness, but great strength. I want to take the time to commend those that are seeking help with the resources God has given to you! The first step to gaining freedom is to humble yourself and ask for help! From God first to guide you on a path of healthy living. Then in no specific order: a support group, from a therapist, from pastor, from church family, from family, from medication. In order to get help you must humble yourself and admit there is a problem, an issue that is out of sorts in your life that does not measure up to your beliefs and values. The fact is that your struggle with whatever mental health issue you are dealing with has left you captivated and struggling. To admit that IS STRENGTH!!! Not weakness!!! (If anyone makes you feel that you are weak, cannot make decisions on our own, constantly questioning your need for help or makes you feel shame, blame and guilt for seeking help then place that person in God's hands and exit the relationship!!! These people could be friends, doctors, family, etc. Take the time to seek out doctors, friends, and loved ones who will listen and be supportive.) Living without support is not healthy and it can only keep you in a state of not getting help. Do not be ashamed of needing medication to survive. I am a true believer that God gave humans the knowledge and ability to help those in need of medication and physical ailments. If God did not intend us to use medicine and physicians for help then He would not have given us the ability to pursue them! I have had great success with using medicine in order to help slow down my thought process so I can process things, but I have also taken great advantage of seeking help from others to break down my thought process to gain some freedom.

> ***Luke 5:31*** *And Jesus answering said unto them, they that are whole need not a physician; but they that are sick.*

> ***Mark 2:17*** *When Jesus heard it, he saith unto them, they that are whole have no need of the physician, but they that are sick: I came not to call the righteous, but sinners to repentance.*

> ***Matthew 9:12-13*** *But when Jesus heard that, he said unto them, they that be whole need not a physician, but they that are sick. But go ye and learn what that meaneth, I will have mercy, and not sacrifice: for I am not come to call the righteous, but sinners to repentance.*

> ***2 Chronicles 16:12*** *And Asa in the thirty and ninth year of his reign was diseased in his feet, until his disease was exceeding great: yet in his disease he sought not to the LORD, but to the physicians.*

> ***Proverbs 17:22*** *A merry heart doeth good like a medicine: but a broken spirit drieth the bones.*

Notice the verses that talk about the need of physician. We distinguish if there is a need of a physician. Is there a struggle with an illness? Jesus said that he did not come to those who were whole, but for those who were in need of healing. Jesus came to heal the issue of death of our soul, of us being born into our sinful nature. Foremost in the healing process is to define what that relationship with God is, and again we are back to our beliefs. Second, if we have sought the Lord for our healing of death to our soul, then we can approach him with other ailments. With that comes the trust in the Lord to help you know when a physician is needed for your issues. I believe that the soul and the body work together in the process of healing. Because one can have an effect on the other. What good does it do ourselves to heal the body but not the mind or spirit? Or heal the spirit but not the body. They go together. I can remember a time when we could go to two doctors and get the answers we needed. One was our pastor and the other was our family doctor. As our world has evolved that has changed in great degrees. Now you have to make an appointment with your pastor, or deacon, or another member of the congregation if it's a large church in order to get help. Then, if you go to the family doctor, they can no longer treat you for anything other than the common cold or flu. Everything else that is suspected is handed out to another "specialist". This then requires a long drawn out process of waiting for appointments and tests and getting worked in, only to be treated as cattle in a long line of other waiting cattle. When their tests and appointments of just talking don't turn anything up, they pass you onto another "specialist" and the process continues. We can wait weeks, months, and even years for help. But as we see here in our verses, the women with many issues of physicians and many issues of blood also spent 12 years in hope of an answer. But the point is that she never gave up hope! She searched, she looked, she took the step to say, 'YES! There is something wrong.' By doing this she gave us the opportunity to not feel alone and gave us the strength to step out of our comfort zone and say something is not right. Through her faith and through her continued bravery to search she was finally made whole. Not in the way she wanted, but in the way God wanted. So, ask yourself: Is there something going on other than my belief? Maybe you are not sure and need help figuring it out. Are you going to pray and seek help from God and others He has put into your life or stay where you are? There is help out there for you!

> ***Jeremiah 8:22*** *Is there no balm in Gilead; is there no physician there? why then is not the health of the daughter of my people recovered?*

> ***Ezekiel 47:12*** *And by the river upon the bank thereof, on this side and on that side, shall grow all trees for meat, whose leaf shall not fade, neither shall the fruit thereof be consumed: it shall bring forth new fruit according to his months, because their waters they issued out of the sanctuary: and the fruit thereof shall be for meat, and the leaf thereof for medicine.*

> ***Ezekiel 27:17*** *Judah, and the land of Israel, they were thy merchants: they traded in thy market wheat*

of Minnith, and Pannag, and honey, and oil, and balm.

<u>Jeremiah 46:11</u> *Go up into Gilead, and take balm, O virgin, the daughter of Egypt: in vain shalt thou use many medicines; for thou shalt not be cured.*

<u>Jeremiah 51:8</u> *Babylon is suddenly fallen and destroyed: howl for her; take balm for her pain, if so be she may be healed.*

<u>Genesis 50:2</u> *And Joseph commanded his servants the physicians to embalm his father: and the physicians embalmed Israel.*

Then we see the verses of physician, medicine, and balm used for healing. Balm is referred to as sap or the process of distillation for the purpose of extracting medicine from plants. Doctor is listed in three verses in the Bible (Luke 2:46, Luke 5:17, and Acts 5:34), but the definition is that of a teacher of the Law. Another word in the Bible is sorcerer. It appears eight times in the Bible and is listed with having the following definition: a person who practices magic, an Oriental wiseman, a false prophet, dream interpreters, use witchcraft, whisper a spell, enchant or practice magic, to mix potions, and medicine for the intent of a spell. There are some translations of the Bible that say it refers to pharmaceuticals and that all pharmacy related medications are bad. But again, you need to have ample proof of these references throughout the Bible and there is not one to represent this theory. I would say the purpose of a mixing medication is the actual purpose and motif that needs to be examined. Is one using it for the purpose of casting a spell, or is one using it for the purpose of healing? What is the motive behind the heart? God and us can only be the two who can search this answer as we have discussed. To move on we see here that these verses talk of medicine and balm for healing. We can find these medicines in the trees and plants that live among us. God has given some of us the gift of healing. Paul who had all spiritual gifts talks to us ...

> **1 Corinthians 12** *Now concerning spiritual gifts, brethren, I would not have you ignorant. Ye know that ye were Gentiles, carried away unto these dumb idols, even as ye were led. Wherefore I give you to understand, that no man speaking by the Spirit of God calleth Jesus accursed: and that no man can say that Jesus is the Lord, but by the Holy Ghost. Now there are diversities of gifts, but the same Spirit And there are differences of administrations, but the same Lord. And there are diversities of operations, but it is the same God which worketh all in all. <u>But the manifestation of the Spirit is given to every man to profit withal. For to one is given by the Spirit the word of wisdom; to another the word of knowledge by the same Spirit; To another faith by the same Spirit; to another the gifts of healing by the same Spirit; to another the working of miracles; to another prophecy; to another discerning of spirits; to another divers kinds of tongues; to another the interpretation of tongues: But all these worketh that one and the selfsame Spirit, dividing to every man severally as he will.</u> For as the body is one, and hath many members, and all the members of that one body, being many, are one body: so also is Christ. For by one Spirit are we all baptized into one body, whether we be Jews or Gentiles, whether we be bond or free; and have been all made to drink into one*

Spirit. For the body is not one member, but many. If the foot shall say, Because I am not the hand, I am not of the body; is it therefore not of the body? And if the ear shall say, Because I am not the eye, I am not of the body; is it therefore not of the body? If the whole body were an eye, where were the hearing? If the whole were hearing, where were the smelling? But now hath God set the members every one of them in the body, as it hath pleased him. And if they were all one member, where were the body? But now are they many members, yet but one body. And the eye cannot say unto the hand, I have no need of thee: nor again the head to the feet, I have no need of you. Nay, much more those members of the body, which seem to be more feeble, are necessary: And those members of the body, which we think to be less honourable, upon these we bestow more abundant honour; and our uncomely parts have more abundant comeliness. For our comely parts have no need: but God hath tempered the body together, having given more abundant honour to that part which lacked: That there should be no schism in the body; but that the members should have the same care one for another. And whether one member suffer, all the members suffer with it; or one member be honoured, all the members rejoice with it. Now ye are the body of Christ, and members in particular. And God hath set some in the church, first apostles, secondarily prophets, thirdly teachers, after that miracles, then gifts of healings, helps, governments, diversities of tongues. Are all apostles? are all prophets? are all teachers? are all workers of miracles? Have all the gifts of healing? do all speak with tongues? do all

*interpret? But covet earnestly the best gifts: and yet
shew I unto you a more excellent way.*

These verses again give such great clarity it amazes me. Upon
our confession of Faith in God we are sent the Holy Spirit, and
with the Holy spirit we each have individual gifts. These gifts are
given to help in the furthering building of Faith and spreading
the word of God. And among them is the gift to heal. Plain and
simple. There are those of us who have the gift to help others who
need healing. Whether it be a healing of the spirit, or healing of
the body, but more importantly this passage goes on to tell us that
we are consistent with many members and all members are in
need of each other. When one member suffer so does the other. In
truth He is talking in a parable about the church, but the example
of the body is a true characteristic of the body we tend to not
acknowledge. Our proof the soul is part of the body. The soul is a
member of the body and is needed in order for it to work. When
one member is affected, they are all affected. If your mind, spirit,
soul, and heart are affected then the body will be affected so why
would you not look to heal it.

> ***Matthew 4:24*** *And his fame went throughout all
> Syria: and they brought unto him all sick people that
> were taken with divers diseases and torments, and
> those which were possessed with devils, and those
> which were lunatick, and those that had the palsy;
> and he healed them.*

> ***Matthew 17:15*** *Lord, have mercy on my son: for he
> is lunatick, and sore vexed: for ofttimes he falleth into
> the fire, and oft into the water.*

Lunatic: To be moonstruck, crazy. To be epileptic which increases with the increase of the moon.

Understand that there are many actual illnesses that are related to the mind. The bible talks of it using the word lunatic. Not the most politically correct word in the English language and society, but look at the verses and the definition. I am more than sure there was not much knowledge of epilepsy in Biblical times, but there were cases of it. Many great names of history struggled with diseases of the mind. Julius Caesar suffered from epilepsy, King George III suffered with polyuria, Harriet Tubman had narcolepsy, Samuel Johnson had Tourette's syndrome, Jane Austin had Addison's Disease, Abraham Lincoln had depression, Winston Churchill had bipolar disorder. There were also people of the Bible who experienced mental health struggles:

David There are so many scriptures that talk about his anguish, his fear, his lack of sleep. His Psalms were laced with anguish, yet he always tried to concentrate on the hope of God. Yet, his anguish was real! (1 Samuel 30:4–6, Psalm 102)

Elijah He begged the Lord to take his life, the battle was too much for him to bare any longer. An angel came and took care over him because he was unable to do it himself. (1 Kings 19:4–5.)

Hannah She laid and wept day and night and could not stop. She could not eat. This reminds me at times when my depression is so great. The mental pain is so strong that the body just shuts itself down and emotions just role in a constant sea of turmoil. (1 Samuel 1:7–10).

Paul He talks of his peril in Asia. When they were in such despair they feared for their life. They felt hopeless and out of strength. (2 Corinthians 1:8–10)

Jesus He anguished so much before he was crucified on the cross. He went to the garden and prayed multiple times for God to take the burden of sacrifice from him. HE anguished so much his sweat turned to blood. (Luke 22:41–44)

There are many more cases of illness and disease in the Bible. So many Jesus spent a lot of his ministry healing people of all various issues. Issues that affect both the body and the mind. The one thing all these people had in common is they sought the Lord for help. Or a member of their family did!

When I was at my worst moment the last thing I could do was reach out to God. The pressure of beliefs was so overwhelming I could not handle it. I admitted this to God and then asked Him to carry me until I could get to a point of reaching for Him. He loved me just as much in that moment as He did when I reached for Him. When I could not pray myself, I had a support group who did it for me! Is that not amazing? My name was ever constantly brought to the Lord through people whose faith was stronger than mine was at that moment.

Music

("All This Time" by Britt Nicole)
("Praying" by Keesha)
("Up to The Mountain" by Kelly Clarkson)
("You Raise Me Up" by Josh Groban)
("Better Hands Now" by Natalie Grant)

("You Got This" by Lindsey Gort)

("Clean" by Natalie Grant)

("The God I Know" by Love & the Outcome) ("Broken" by Lifehouse) ("Grace" by Laura Story) ("He's A Chain Breaker" by Zach Williams)

Conclusion

Living by faith is a process of taking each step of your day to practice living in the joy of knowing God is in control until it comes so natural to you it does not require the same effort as when you first began. A journey of obstacles causing ups and downs that will try to throw you off your path and make you stumble or set you back. But you continue to get back up and learn from the ups and downs and pursue your faith until the very end. A daily process of hoping, trusting, and keeping your faith. It's the work field: the battle field.

The hardest thing I have found is mental health disorders can make faith seem like an impossible task. It affects the part of our mind that has faith, security, belief, and confidence and turns it down so it seems impossible and hopeless to get it turned back on. I have found with medication, help from support, doctors who listen, and continued growth in the knowledge of God it has been turned on. It does not always stay at the level I wish it to, but with each incident it restores my hope and faith that each moment is only temporary and better days are possible and ahead of me. That God's love for me is constant and never changing! David committed murder, adultery, loss of a child, was attempted to be killed by his Uncle, and his son, and responsible for his kingdom of people who hated him at times. Yet, he kept the faith. He anguished, he suffered, he feared, he sinned on purpose for self-gratification, but God loved him the same. He delivered him! He brought him through to be a great king, he had a son who followed in his footsteps as king (King Solomon), and he was granted great wisdom. All that we go through and all that we struggle with all comes back to one thing and that is belief. When we have expectations, time, thoughts, balance, illness, judgement, pressure, and condemnation. All these yokes point back to: what do you believe? Find out what you believe and spend your time living it!

My point here is please seek help. Please do not be ashamed of taking medicine, talking with someone, depending on help from others. The Lord is there waiting patiently for you to ask for help. Seek it and let Him guide you. Search for someone who will support you in what you believe and not what they want you to believe. Mental health is not a spiritual issue, but a body issue, part of a unit that makes up a whole. But with the help of balancing spiritual, mental, emotional, and physical, you can have great moments of peace. Carry this cross you bear with hope, trust, and acceptance. It's not about a cure to go around it, but the tools you need to go through it. God made you specifically as you are and He trusts you to reach out to Him when the time it right. You have the power to be as close to him as you want or as far away from Him as you want. Regardless of your choice, He will love you the same. His grace (love) will stand and not waiver as the world does. His standards will not change like the world's does. He is constant. He is love! So, keep the Faith, grow and never lose hope!

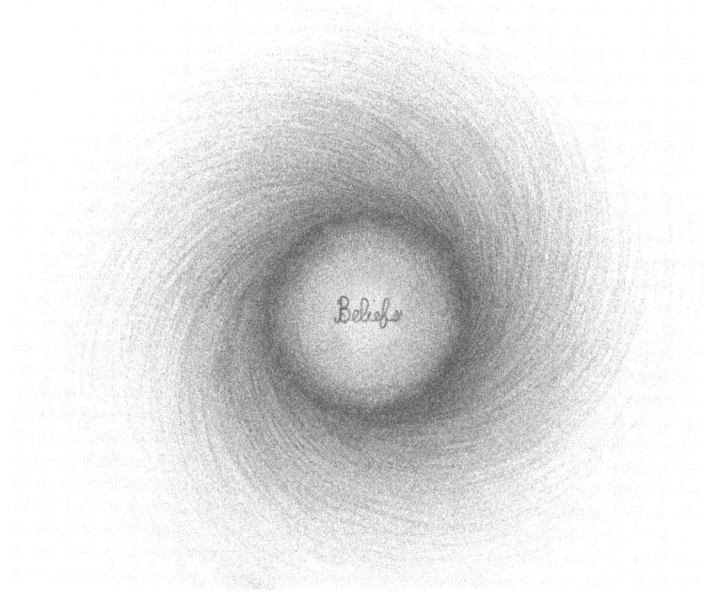

II Timothy 4:7 I have fought a good fight, I have finished my course, I have kept the faith.

Music

("Tell Your Heart to Beat Again" by Danny Goke)
("Fight Song" by Rachel Platten)
("Stand Back Up" by Sugarland)
("Once and for All" by Lauren Daigle)
("Not for A Moment" by Meredith Andrews)
("Just Be Held" by Casting Crowns)
("One Step Away" by Casting Crowns)

Jesus Life on Earth

Jesus experienced temptation:

Matthew 4:1-11 *"Then was Jesus led up of the Spirit into the wilderness to be tempted of the devil. And when he had fasted forty days and forty nights, he was afterward an hungred. And when the tempter came to him, he said, if thou be the Son of God, command that these stones be made bread. But he answered and said, it is written, Man shall not live by bread alone, but by every word that proceedeth out of the mouth of God. Then the devil taketh him up into the holy city, and setteth him on a pinnacle of the temple, And saith unto him, If thou be the Son of God, cast thyself down: for it is written, He shall give his angels charge concerning thee: and in their hands they shall bear thee up, lest at any time thou dash thy foot against a stone. Jesus said unto him, it is written again, Thou shalt not tempt the Lord thy God. Again, the devil taketh him up into an exceeding high mountain, and sheweth him all the kingdoms of the world, and the glory of them; And saith unto him, all these things will I give thee, if thou wilt fall down and worship me. Then saith Jesus unto him, get thee hence, Satan: for it is written, Thou shalt worship the Lord thy God, and him only shalt* *thou serve. Then the devil leaveth him, and, behold, angels came and ministered unto him."*

Matthew 27:38-44 *Then were there two thieves crucified with him, one on the right hand, and another on the left. And they that passed by reviled him, wagging their heads, and saying, Thou that destroyest the temple, and buildest it in three days, save thyself. If thou be the Son of God, come down from the cross. Likewise also the chief priests mocking him, with the scribes and elders, said, He saved others; himself he cannot save. If he be the King of Israel, let him now come down from the cross, and we will believe him. He trusted in God; let him deliver him now, if he will have him: for he said, I am the Son of God. The thieves also, which were crucified with him, cast the same in his teeth.*

Jesus experienced suffering, anguish, loneliness, being bullied and Slandered:

Luke 22:63-65 *And the men that held Jesus mocked him, and smote him. And when they had blindfolded him, they struck him on the face, and asked him, saying, Prophesy, who is it that smote thee? And many other things blasphemously spake they against him.*

John 19 *"Then Pilate therefore took Jesus, and scourged him. And the soldiers platted a crown of thorns, and put it on his head, and they put on him a purple robe, and said, Hail, King of the Jews! and they smote him with their hands. Pilate therefore went* *forth again, and saith unto them, Behold, I bring him forth to you, that ye may know that I find no fault in him. Then came Jesus forth, wearing the crown of thorns, and the purple robe. And Pilate saith unto them, Behold the man! When the chief priests therefore and officers saw him, they cried out, saying, crucify him, crucify him. Pilate saith unto them, take ye him, and crucify him: for I find no fault in him. The Jews answered him, we have a law, and by our law he ought to die, because he made himself the Son of God. When Pilate therefore heard that saying, he was the more afraid; And went again into the judgment hall, and saith unto Jesus, Whence art thou? But Jesus gave him no answer. Then saith Pilate unto him, Speakest thou not unto me? knowest thou not that I have power to crucify thee, and have power to release thee? Jesus answered, Thou couldest have no power at all against me, except it were given thee from above: therefore he that delivered me unto thee hath the greater sin. And from thenceforth Pilate sought to release him: but the Jews cried out, saying, if thou let this man go, thou art not Caesar's friend: whosoever maketh himself a king speaketh against Caesar. When Pilate therefore heard that saying, he brought Jesus forth, and sat down in the judgment seat in a place that is called the Pavement, but in the Hebrew, Gabbatha. And it was the preparation of the passover, and about the sixth hour: and he saith unto the Jews, Behold your King! But they cried out, away with him, away with him, crucify him. Pilate saith unto them, Shall I crucify your King? The chief priests answered, we have no king but Caesar. Then delivered he him therefore unto them to be crucified. And they took Jesus, and led him away. And he bearing his cross went forth into a place called the place of a skull, which is called in the Hebrew Golgotha: Where they crucified him, and two other with him, on either side one, and Jesus in the midst. And Pilate wrote a title, and put it on the cross. And the writing was* Jesus Of Nazareth The King Of The Jews. *This title then read many of the Jews: for the place where Jesus was crucified was nigh to the city: and it was written in Hebrew, and Greek, and Latin. Then said the chief priests of the Jews to Pilate, write not, The King of the Jews; but that he said, I am King of the Jews. Pilate answered, What I have written I have written. Then the soldiers, when they had crucified Jesus, took his garments, and made four parts, to every soldier a part; and also, his coat: now the coat was without seam, woven from the top throughout. They said therefore among themselves, let us not rend it, but cast lots for it, whose it shall be: that the scripture might be fulfilled, which saith, they parted my raiment among them, and for my vesture they did cast lots. These things therefore the soldiers did. Now there stood by the cross of Jesus his mother, and his mother's sister, Mary the wife of Cleophas, and Mary Magdalene. When Jesus therefore saw his mother, and the disciple standing by, whom he loved, he saith unto his mother, Woman, behold thy son! Then saith he to the disciple, Behold thy mother! And from that hour that disciple took her unto his own home. After this, Jesus knowing that all things were now accomplished, that the scripture might be fulfilled, saith, I thirst. Now there was set a vessel full of vinegar: and they filled a spunge with vinegar, and put it upon hyssop, and put it to his mouth. When Jesus therefore had received the vinegar, he said, It is finished: and he bowed his head, and gave up the ghost. The Jews therefore, because it was the preparation, that the bodies should not remain upon the cross on the sabbath day, (for that sabbath day was a high day,) besought Pilate that their legs might be broken, and that they might be taken away. Then came the soldiers, and brake the legs of the first, and of the other which was crucified with him. But when they came to Jesus, and saw that he was dead already, they brake not his legs: But one of the soldiers with a spear pierced his side, and forthwith came there out blood and water. And he that saw it bare record, and his record is true: and he knoweth that he saith true, that ye might believe. For these things were done, that the scripture should be fulfilled, A bone of him shall not be broken. And again, another scripture saith, they shall look on him whom they pierced.*

Matthew 27:27-31 *Then released he Barabbas unto them: and when he had scourged Jesus, he delivered him to be crucified. Then the soldiers of the governor took Jesus into the common hall, and gathered unto him the whole band of soldiers. And they stripped him, and put on him a scarlet robe. And when they had platted a crown of thorns, they put it upon his head, and a reed in his right hand: and they bowed the knee before him, and mocked him, saying, Hail, King of the Jews! And they spit upon him, and took the reed, and smote him on the head. And after that* *they had mocked him, they took the robe off from him, and put his own raiment on him, and led him away to crucify him.*

Matthew 27:45-49 *Now from the sixth hour there was darkness over all the land unto the ninth hour. And about the ninth hour Jesus cried with a loud voice, saying, Eli, Eli, lama sabachthani? that is to say, My God, my God, why hast thou forsaken me? Some of them that stood there, when they heard that, said, This man calleth for Elias. And straightway one of them ran, and took a spunge, and filled it with vinegar, and put it on a reed, and gave him to drink. The rest said, let be, let us see whether Elias will come to save him. Jesus, when he had cried again with a loud voice, yielded up the ghost.*

Jesus experienced depression, anxiety, great sorrow, anguish, despair, a heavy heart, and became withdrawn:

Luke 22:40-46 *"And when he was at the place, he said unto them, pray that ye enter not into temptation. And he was withdrawn from them about a stone's cast, and kneeled down, and prayed, Saying, Father, if thou be willing, remove this cup from me: nevertheless, not my will, but thine, be done. And there appeared an angel unto him from heaven, strengthening him. And being in an agony he prayed more earnestly: and his sweat was as it were great drops of blood falling down to the ground. And when he rose up from prayer, and was come to his disciples, he found them sleeping*

*for sorrow, and said unto them, why sleep ye? rise and
pray, lest ye enter into temptation"*

Hematidrosis is a rare, but very real, medical condition where
one's sweat will contain blood. The sweat glands are surrounded
by tiny blood vessels. These vessels can constrict and then dilate
to the point of rupture where the blood will then effuse into the
sweat glands. Its cause? —*extreme* anguish.

> ***Matthew 26:36-39*** *Then cometh Jesus with them
> unto a place called Gethsemane, and saith unto the
> disciples, sit ye here, while I go and pray yonder. And
> he took with him Peter and the two sons of Zebedee,
> and began to be sorrowful and very heavy. Then
> saith he unto them, my soul is exceeding sorrowful,
> even unto death: tarry ye here, and watch with me.
> And he went a little farther, and fell on his face,
> and prayed, saying, O my Father, if it be possible,
> let this cup pass from me: nevertheless, not as I will,
> but as thou wilt*

> ***Mark 14:32-36*** *And they came to a place which was
> named Gethsemane: and he saith to his disciples, sit
> ye here, while I shall pray. And he taketh with him
> Peter and James and John, and began to be sore
> amazed, and to be very heavy; And saith unto them,
> my soul is exceeding sorrowful unto death: tarry
> ye here, and watch. And he went forward a little,
> and fell on the ground, and prayed that, if it were
> possible, the hour might pass from him. And he said,
> Abba, Father, all things are possible unto thee; take*

away this cup from me: nevertheless, not what I will, but what thou wilt

Jesus experienced anger:

<u>**Mark 11:15-19**</u> *"And they come to Jerusalem: and Jesus went into the temple, and began to cast out them that sold and bought in the temple, and overthrew the tables of the moneychangers, and the seats of them that sold doves; And would not suffer that any man should carry* any *vessel through the temple. And he taught, saying unto them, is it not written, my house shall be called of all nations the house of prayer? but ye have made it a den of thieves. And the scribes and chief priests heard* it, *and sought how they might destroy him: for they feared him, because all the people was astonished at his doctrine. And when even was come, he went out of the city"*

<u>**John 2:11-20**</u> *"This beginning of miracles did Jesus in Cana of Galilee, and manifested forth his glory; and his disciples believed on him. After this he went down to Capernaum, he, and his mother, and his brethren, and his disciples: and they continued there not many days. And the Jews' passover was at hand, and Jesus went up to Jerusalem, and found in the temple those that sold oxen and sheep and doves, and the changers of money sitting: And when he had made a scourge of small cords, he drove them all out of the temple, and the sheep, and the oxen; and poured out the changers' money, and overthrew the tables; And said unto them that sold doves, take these things hence; make not*

my Father's house a house of merchandise. And his disciples remembered that it was written, the zeal of thine house hath eaten me up. Then answered the Jews and said unto him, what sign shewest thou unto us, seeing that thou doest these things? Jesus answered and said unto them, destroy this temple, and in three days I will raise it up. Then said the Jews, Forty and six years was this temple in building, and wilt thou rear it up in three days? But he spake of the temple of his body"

Jesus experienced acceptance:

__Matthew 27:11-14__ And Jesus stood before the governor: and the governor asked him, saying, Art thou the King of the Jews? And Jesus said unto him, Thou sayest. And when he was accused of the chief priests and elders, he answered nothing. Then said Pilate unto him, Hearest thou not how many things they witness against thee? And he answered him to never a word; insomuch that the governor marvelled greatly.

__Mark 15:1-5__ And as soon as it was morning the chief priests, with the elders and scribes, and the whole council held a consultation, and they bound Jesus and led him away and delivered him to Pilate. And Pilate asked him, "Are you the King of the Jews?" And he answered him "You have said so." And the chief priests accused him of many things. And Pilate again asked him, "Have you no answer to make? See how many charges they bring against you." But Jesus made no further answer, so that Pilate wondered.

__Luke 23:1-12__ Then the whole company of them arose, and brought him before Pilate. And they began to accuse him, saying, `We found this man perverting our nation, and forbidding us to give tribute to Caesar, and saying that he himself is Christ a king." And Pilate asked him, "Are you the King of the Jews?" And he answered him. "You have said so. "And Pilate said to the chief priests and the multitudes, I find no crime in this man. "But they were urgent, saying, `He stirs up the people, teaching throughout all Judea, from Galilee even to this place. When Pilate heard this, he asked whether the man was a Galilean. And when he learned that he belonged to Herod's jurisdiction, he sent him over to Herod, who was himself in Jerusalem at that time. When Herod saw Jesus, he was very glad, for he had long desired to see him, because he had heard about him, and he was hoping to see some sign done by him. So, he questioned him at some length, but he made no answer. The chief priests and the scribes stood by, vehemently accusing him. And Herod with his soldiers treated him with contempt and mocked him; then, arraying him in gorgeous apparel, he sent him back to Pilate. And Herod and Pilate became friends with each other that very day, for before this they had been at enmity with each other.

__John 18:28-38__ Then they led Jesus from the house of Caiaphas to the praetorium. It was early. They themselves did not enter the praetorium, so that they might not be defiled, but might eat the Passover. So, Pilate went out to them and said, "What accusation do you bring against this man?" They answered him,

"If this man were not an evildoer, we would not have handed him over." Pilate said to them, "Take him yourselves and judge him by your own law." The Jews said to him "it is not lawful for us to put any man to death." This was to fulfil the word which Jesus had spoken to show by what death he was to die. Pilate entered the praetorium again and called Jesus, and said to him, "Are you the King of the Jews?" Jesus answered, "Do you say this of your own accord, or did others say it to you about me?' Pilate answered, "Am I a Jew? Your own nation and the chief priests have handed you over to me; what have you done?" Jesus answered, "My kingship is not of this world; if my kingship were of this world, my servants would fight, that I might not be handed over to the Jews, but my kingship is not from the world." Pilate said to him, "So you are a king?" Jesus answered. "You say that I am a king. For this I was born, and for this I have come into the world, to bear witness to the truth. Everyone who is of the truth hears my voice," Pilate said to him, "What is truth?" After he had said this, he went out to the Jews again, and told them, "I find no crime in him".

Jesus accepted his fate on the cross. He shows this by not fighting Pilate, the priest, or the people. He doesn't give up; He doesn't try to take control of the situation; He doesn't try to change the minds of those around him; He chooses to be still and go through the suffering that is before him, and trust the outcome.

Is God a Fair God?

__Psalm 25:7-10__ Remember not the sins of my youth, nor my transgressions: according to thy mercy remember thou me for thy goodness' sake, O LORD. __Good and upright is__ __the LORD:__ therefore will he teach sinners in the way. The meek will he guide in judgment: and the meek will he teach his way. All the paths of the LORD are mercy and truth unto such as keep his covenant and his testimonies.

__Psalms 116:1-8__ Because he hath inclined his ear unto me, therefore will I call upon him as long as I live. The sorrows of death compassed me, and the pains of hell gat hold upon me: I found trouble and sorrow. Then called I upon the name of the LORD; O LORD, I beseech thee, deliver my soul. __Gracious__ __is the LORD, and righteous; yea, our God is merciful.__ The LORD preserveth the simple: I was brought low, and he helped me. Return unto thy rest, O my soul; for the LORD hath dealt bountifully with thee. For thou hast delivered my soul from death, mine eyes from tears, and my feet from falling

---

You may be asking yourself how could God be so cruel as to let us experience this. Well, let me ask you this… Would you prefer a God who dictates your every move, emotion, thoughts, and actions? Or, would you prefer to have free will? God did not want a puppet for a friend, instead, he wanted a being who chose to want to know Him. The true foundation of any relationship requires participation from both parties. This is required for the relationship to grow, nourish, and become something great and close. But what we often miss here is how God also protected us and gave us ways to overcome this knowledge of evil. He prepared a path for us so let's look at that.

> **_Genesis 3:22-24_** *"And the Lord God said, Behold, the man is become as one of us, to know good and evil: and now, lest he put forth his hand, and take also of the tree of life, and eat, and live forever: Therefore the Lord God sent him forth from the garden of Eden. To till the ground from whence he was taken. So, he drove out the man; and he placed at the east of the garden of Eden Cherubims, and a flaming sword which turned every way, to keep the way of the tree of life."*

> **_John 3:16_** *"For God so loved the world that He gave His Only Son, that whosoever believeth in Him should not perish but have every lasting life"*

> **_Romans 8:28_** *"And we know that all things work together for good to them that love God, to them who are the called according to his purpose"*

I know as I recall the story of Adam and Eve that I believed that they were kicked out of the garden because they ate the fruit that God told them not to. The verses here show us this is not the case. The Lord sent Adam and Eve out of the garden to protect them. There were two trees in the center of the garden they were not to eat from. One was the tree of knowledge of good and evil.

The second was the tree of life. If they were to eat from the tree of life, they would live forever. God sent them out of the garden to keep this from happening. If they ate of the tree while knowing good and evil then they would have been forever stuck with the struggle of life without death. Instead, God sent them out, sent His son to sacrifice his perfect being, and then promised that if we follow Him to make all this evil knowledge turn out for our good. That is amazing! That is grace!

Adam and Eve ate of the fruit for the promise to become like gods. The thought was planted that they were being left out, not measuring up to their full potential. A thought that left them believing that they were being lied to. Instead of asking the question, where is this coming from? Is this accurate? They moved on making a decision with complete trust. They disobeyed a direct command from God. I am a true believer that God does not look on the type of sin or categorize each and every sin on a scale from good to bad. I believe that God looks on the motive of the heart behind that sin. (1 Sam 16:7, Proverbs 16:2, Isaiah 55:8,9, and Romans 8:27) What was their heart and mind contemplating when they made this decision? This is why the mind and heart are so precious. God says in *Proverbs 4:23, "Keep thy heart with all diligence; for out of it are the issues of life."* Keep means to guard, watch, and preserve.

So, what are you doing to protect your heart and mind? Do you ride the train of thought every time it comes your way? Are you drowning yourself in alcohol and/or drugs to avoid the pain, to escape the fears that come? Are you convinced there is nothing wrong with you? Can you admit you need help and cannot overcome this on your own? Are you being prideful and stubborn and want God to skip through these processes to the end because it's not fair and you don't deserve this? Or, do you have faith that there is hope and a way that this journey can be a learning experience full of promise and peace?

I encourage you to face your fears, make that move to guard and strengthen your heart, and move past whatever it is that has you stuck and go! Trust that God will help you and use this journey to strengthen you, make you stronger, and reward you for your faith and trust in Him. You are not alone, and if you reach out for God, He will show you a path and guide you to become confident and whole again!

Music

("I Surrender" by Blanca)
("Greater Is He" by Blanca)
("The River" by Hillary Scott)

The Punishment of Adam and Eve

What kind of God would He be if He was not fair? If He punished this person, but not that one? If He put a scale to our sins of measure how good or how bad it was. **God does not do this**. The action is what it is. It either has a profitable, agreeable result, or a malignant, hurtful result. To make sure we have the full story let's discover what their punishment truly was.

> ___Genesis 3:14-19___ *"And the Lord God said unto the <u>serpent,</u> because thou hast done this, thou are cursed above all cattle, and above every beast of the fieled; upon thy belly shalt thou go, and dust shalt thou eat all the days of thy life: And I will put enmity between thee and the woman, and between thy seed and her seed; it shall bruise thy head, and thou shalt bruise his heel. Unto the <u>woman</u> he said, I will greatly multiply thy sorrow and thy conception; in sorrow thou shalt bring forth children; and thy desire shall be to thy husband, and he shall rule over thee. And unto <u>Adam</u> he said, because thou has hearkened unto the voice of thy wife, and hast eaten of the tree, of which I commanded thee saying, Thou shalt not ear of it; cursed is the ground for the sake; in sorrow shalt thou eat of it all the days*

of thy life; Thorns also and thistles shall it bring forth to thee; and thou shalt eat the herb of the field; In the sweat of thy face shalt thou eat bread, till thou return unto the ground; for out of it wast thou taken: for dust thou art, and unto dust shalt thou return."

We have three distinct characters that were involved: Adam, Eve, and the serpent.

The serpent was the most beautiful and graceful creature God had made. I think this is a symbolism to remind us that often situations come to us in a beautiful, graceful manner that is enticing and full of promises, purposely making it hard to know which path to take. Because of the serpent allowing Satan to use him the whole animal kingdom was affected. (Jeremiah 12:4, Romans 8:20) The Serpent was to slither on his belly and eat dust for the rest of his life, instead of walking upright. Next, God would make an enemy of Satan and the woman, that God would make a spiritual barrier between Satan and the woman, leading to the division between Satan's people and God's people. Then the seed of the woman (a child) would lead to the death blow to Satan. By the sacrifice of the seed (a perfect child of God) would lead to Jesus bruising on the cross and the crushing of Satan and his kingdom.

The woman would receive sorrow and conception. No longer would man be created, but man would create man. In so doing this, pain would be involved and the dependency woman would have on man became her desire. With this desire came the struggle. Some say her natural desire to submit to man would be a burden, yet others would say the desire not to submit would be her burden. I believe it is both! (To defile the body in any way is considered a sin. With God's creation of Adam and Eve before the eating of the tree, there was no need for the body to be pressed upon or in dependency upon for offspring. This is also a symbol that we are born to sin. One's body would have to be compromised for us to be born, thus we are born in sin, of sin. If God would have created us Himself, we would not be born in sin but in His perfect image. Hand touched by God, the most holy and perfect one, would leave us that way.)

Man would share equally with the woman and have sorrow. No longer would he eat from the food of the trees that was freely provided. Now He would eat from the ground. He will have to work and toil all the days of his life, with the ground and thorns and thistles growing and making it harder for him.

> **Genesis 3:21** *"Unto Adam also and his wife did the Lord God make coats of skins, and clothed them."*

Never before had a living creature been killed, but the Lord sacrificed the animal to make clothes for Adam and Eve. Thus, the blood sacrifice was required to cover the shame, guilt, and fear of their sin. This became the process of forgiveness.

What I find so amazing in all of this is even though we have punishment and consequences for our thoughts that lead to actions, the Lord will not only forgive us, but promises us there is hope. He is fair in his punishment, giving us at times what we deserve, equal punishment. But with faith in Him, He opened up an opportunity for us to experience mercy and grace, with justice.

Justice	Mercy	Grace
Getting what you deserve	Not getting what you deserve	Getting something, you don't deserve and more
Romans 6:23- For the wages of sin is death	But the gift of God is eternal life	Through Jesus Christ our Lord
Our cost, our justice, of being born in our sinful nature is death. To die without hope of anything more than sorrow and pain.	God, decided to have mercy on us and provide a way for us to have eternal life with peace and happiness. No more sorrow, no more pain.	Instead of making us pay that sacrifice He sent His perfect son who did nothing wrong to sacrifice His life, body, and soul for us when we don't deserve it. The greatest of all Loves! That is Grace!

The hope with our faith in Him that it will all turn out for good in the end. We may have this yoke around our necks of the struggle between light and dark, but God in return gave us the opportunity to acknowledge the light and dark, asks for His forgiveness, and seek His help. He did not leave us to our own accord, but gave us the opportunity to choose Him and gave us a new path to get to Him.

Music

("Loyal" by Lauren Daigle)
("I Can Just Be Me" by Laura Story)

Parable of the Sower

The Rocks, Thorns and Thistles in the Field

Matthew 13:1-23 and Mark 3:1-20 *The same day went Jesus out of the house, and sat by the sea side. And great multitudes were gathered together unto him, so that he went into a ship, and sat; and the whole multitude stood on the shore. And he spake many things unto them in parables, saying, Behold, a sower went forth to sow; And when he sowed, some seeds fell by the way side, and the fowls came and devoured them up: Some fell upon stony places, where they had not much earth: and forthwith they sprung up, because they had no deepness of earth: And when the sun was up, they were scorched; and because they had no root, they withered away. And some fell among thorns; and the thorns sprung up, and choked them: But other fell into good ground, and brought forth fruit, some a hundredfold, some sixtyfold, some thirtyfold. Who hath ears to hear, let him heart, And the disciples came, and said unto him, Why speakest thou unto them in parables? He answered and said unto them, because it is given unto you to know the mysteries of the kingdom of heaven, but to them it is not given. For whosoever hath, to him* *shall be given, and he shall have more abundance: but whosoever hath not, from him shall be taken away even that he hath. Therefore, speak I to them in parables: because they seeing see not; and hearing they hear not, neither do they understand. And in them is fulfilled the prophecy of Esaias, which saith, by hearing ye shall hear, and shall not understand; and seeing ye shall see, and shall not perceive: For this people's heart is waxed gross, and their ears are dull of hearing, and their eyes they have closed; lest at any time they should see with their eyes and hear with their ears, and should understand with their heart, and should be converted, and I should heal them. But blessed are your eyes, for they see: and your ears, for they hear. For verily I say unto you, that many prophets and righteous men have desired to see those things which ye see, and have not seen them; and to hear those things which ye hear, and have not heard them. Hear ye therefore the parable of the sower. When any one heareth the word of the kingdom, and understandeth it not, then cometh the wicked one, and catcheth away that which was sown in his heart. This is he which received seed by the way side. But he that received the seed into stony places, the same is he that heareth the word, and anon with joy receiveth it, yet hath he not roots in himself, but dureth for a while: for when tribulation or persecution ariseth because of the word, by and by he is offended He also that received seed among the thorns is he that heareth the word; and the care of this world, and the deceitfulness of riches, choke the word, and he becometh unfruitful. But he that*

*received seed into the good ground is he that heareth
the word, and understandeth it; which also beareth
fruit, and bringeth forth, some an hundredfold, some
sixty, some thirty.*

The four types of soil represent four types of people and the
seed is the word of God delivered by a source. One could say the
soil represents the state of a person's heart and mind.

Type and placement of soil	heart and mind of that person	Action
They fell by the way side	unsympathetic, indifferent, cold	Do not react to the word, and Satan comes and steals it away with other thoughts, concerns, or distractions so they do not believe.
Stony ground	spontaneous, impetuous	Believers that respond quickly, but do not take into account the sacrifice and quickly become offended and give up, they have no root.
Among thorns	lost in thought, in a world of their own	Believers that let the cares of the world, money, and power take more importance than God's word and teachings.

Good ground	few people, take to heart	These believers take to heart the word of God, they grow, learn from it, and bear fruit, and grow character traits of the fruit of the spirit. According to their ability God giveth to them. Not a measure of what is standard.

We see here the different types of people that are on this earth. This is not for you to judge and categorize them, but for you to seek where you lay. We have already studied about how we each need to work out our own salvation, our own beliefs. So where are you in this?

What do you believe?

Finding your beliefs and values is a huge part in knowing yourself, where you stand, what bothers you, and what you are not willing to compromise. Knowing what you believe and having that knowledge is powerful in your recovery. This is a big part of having counseling. To help you sort out what you believe and gaining confidence in standing lovingly firm in those beliefs. Now our understanding is constantly growing with life. It's a journey not an instant knowledge. But to help you I will give you a list of questions I asked myself as I began my own journey of recovery. I will also give you my answers. This gave me a basis to grow on and I hope finding your own answers does the same for you:

1) Do you believe in a higher power, creator? Explain.

> Yes, I believe that there is one God. I believe He created this world and all of its beauty, and creatures on purpose. I believe He created it in six days and rested on the seventh and there is a great significance in that. I believe He created man and woman. I believe He is the sole energy source that keeps this world and everything in it moving forward. I believe God has no beginning and no ending. I believe God can be anywhere at any time.

I believe God can be in more than one place at a time. I believe we are born into a sinful nature and body and it is required to acknowledge this and ask for forgiveness (repentance). I believe the price for our sins in the shedding of innocent blood. I believe He sent his perfect innocent son to earth to live and die by sacrifice so it would open up a way for us to live with Him in heaven one day. I believe rejecting this belief or teaching against it can keep you from going to heaven. I believe faith in Christ is followed with action (fruits). I believe every believer will have a different measure of fruits according to their abilities given by God and that there is no standard amount that every believer should reach.

2) What do you value, what is most important to you, your main priorities?

I value, first, my relationship with God. I have not always put this first and struggle putting it first. Then myself because without my stability and health I am not good for anyone, (I AM SECOND) then my family, my husband and children, then my church family, and extended family. I value my relationships most of all. To listen, pray, and edify others with as much love, humility, and care as possible, but holding to my beliefs first and foremost.

3) Do you believe a creator left us to our own devices?

No, I do not believe God left us to struggle in this world alone. I believe upon salvation (belief) God gives us a comforter (Holy Spirit) to dwell in and with us to help us in our daily walk and struggle. The Holy Spirit is an extension of God and His glorious power and love. I believe God possesses a great love we can barely comprehend. A love so extraordinary that just a small glimpse of it leaves us breathless and emotional. I believe the Bible is the true word of God in its entirety. I believe God used 40 different men to help pen the 66 books of the Bible over a period of 1600 years to help us in our understanding of him and this world and how to live and cope. I believe the Bible was written in a way it can be used and associated with any time period. I believe that through earnest prayer we can talk to God and that by studying His word He can reveal the path for us to take.

4) Do you believe there are forces working against us?

Yes, I believe Satan exists. I believe he was created by God as an angel and rebelled against God and his authority and was banished from heaven. I believe when he was banished from heaven, he had followers or other angels that went with him and are known as demons. I believe Satan himself believes in God. I believe Satan's sole purpose is to undermine all things that have to do with God and His authority. I believe Satan has no love for anyone but himself and seeks to destroy everything in his path. I believe Satan is extremely intelligent and cunning. I believe we each have our own unique weaknesses and Satan's is an expert on our weaknesses and uses them to deter us.

5) Do you believe you have a specific calling, spiritual gift, or purpose in this world?

Yes, I believe God made each and every one of us different on purpose. I believe God gave each of us different gifts and talents. I believe God uses our individual uniqueness to help each other grow and to fulfill different roles in His kingdom. I believe we all have intelligence in different areas and expertise.

6) What it that calling, gift, or purpose?

My gifts are teaching, administration, compassion, love, singing, and an intelligence to figure out how things are put together just by looking at a completed project. To take two ideas and put them together and add my own unique touch to it. To figure out how things work, a drive to work, and a need to help. Later in life I found I have a talent for art, drawing, and creating. It wasn't until I suffered with multiple physical illnesses that made singing and working an overwhelming task that I discovered my ability for this. As I grow and mature my talents and even my spiritual gifts have changed.

7) Do you believe in mental illnesses?

> Yes, I believe there is a physical component to mental illness. I believe chemical balance, genetics, environmental factors, and personal life experience can all play a role in different degrees in mental illness. I believe some people have a more general weakness to mental illness because of these components. I believe guilt, shame, blame, and fear are symptoms of mental issues and struggles, not the cause of them. I believe faith will not keep you from experiencing mental illness, but it will get you through it and make you stronger. I believe mental illness is not a sign of demonic presence within a person, but through mental illness Satan uses it as a channel to attack that person personally and on a very deep and intimate level.

8) Do you believe that man has a complete understanding of everything?

> No, I do not think we have a complete understanding of everything. If we did then we would not have struggles or trials. We would not have war. We would not have so many differences. We could see everything for what it was and have extreme clarity. Lastly, we wouldn't need God. Who needs God when you know everything? If we knew everything, we could easily become as Satan did and say, "Who needs God." Or, decide to overtake the world. I believe that we can only see what is in front of us and faith is required to trust God with all that we cannot see or comprehend.

9) Do you believe in judgement and punishment?

Yes, I believe in judgement and punishment, but I believe there is a time and place for each. I believe that judgement comes at an appropriate time and that time is at our physical death. When we die and leave this world, we will face God and be judged according to the things we have and have not done. I believe God's punishment will not be to harm us, but to lovingly guide us. I believe God DOES NOT tempt us. God does not set up a trap to catch us to purposely teach us a lesson. I believe life in this world will automatically present that to each of us. I believe that God is a fair God and He uses tough love when needed. I believe trouble and trials are not a sign of punishment from God, but are just a part of this sinful world that we live in. I believe God can see our life in its entirety. When a struggle or trial allows the building of our character (faith, strength, trust, courage, patience, longsuffering, meekness, humility, love, joy, peace, gentleness, goodness, temperance (self-control) content, wisdom, knowledge) He will have us experience it by going through it. I believe God will take some trials and leave others to the building up of our character. I believe there are consequences for our actions. Both hard and easy consequences. I believe God judges based on the heart of a person, not his stature, actions, or accomplishments. The true heart, motive, and character of each person. I believe this is something only God can truly see and therefore we cannot assume, judge, or condemn another person. I believe our main purpose in this life is to present others with the love of Christ with His help. To edify, build up, encourage, come together with love and respect for each other. I believe the Holy Spirit is the one to convict a person to repentance, we cannot personally do that. We can deliver the message of Christ and the best way is with love, not judgement, not condemnation, but with love. I believe we should hold each other accountable but only in a loving way. Without love there is no God, for God is love. I believe love is the strongest of all spiritual gifts. (1 Corinthians 13:13).

10) Do you believe in predestination?

> I believe God knows us before we are conceived, knows us by who we are. By our character, our hearts. By knowing this, He knows we will accept Him and His ways. I believe we have the free choice to choose God, His ways, His teachings, the path we take in that belief. I believe God knows our ultimate destination, but allows us the choice to choose how we get there. I believe God will use the choices we make to grow our faith, if we allow Him to do so. I believe we can be as close to God as we want to be, but it requires action on our part. *"For we are his workmanship, created in Christ Jesus unto good works, which God hath before ordained that we should walk in them." - Ephesians 2:10.*

11) What does Faith mean to you?

Faith means for me to believe in something I cannot see or comprehend an outcome, but to hope and trust in it with my words, actions, and deeds. To trust God is working when I cannot see and that there are things going on within other people that God is working with that I cannot see and must trust in Him to carry out.

12) What does Love mean to you?

Love is an unconditional, unwavering, patient, kind, forgiving, non-boasting, rejoicing, grateful attitude towards others, or towards you, a carrying of unconditional forgiveness extended at all times.

13) What does honor your father and mother mean to you?

As a mother of a young child I view my sons' honoring of me by respecting my ultimate guidance as protecting and nurturing. As my sons come to be adults, I feel as though that role will change as my sons learn to become more independent. I move from a more ultimate guidance role to a role of advice giver. My sons need to take all I have taught them or didn't teach them and find their way in the world to seek what they believe and hold valuable. I am here to support them as much as I am capable with love and edification. Growing a mutual relationship of honor, love, and respect for each other is the ultimate goal.

14) What does Satan getting a foothold in your life mean to you?

> For this it means I am not a believer in God and I am choosing to do things my way, while rejecting all things of God and His ways. That for Satan to have a hold on me, I am not a child of God and I have not prayed a prayer of salvation.

15) What does black, white, and gray area mean to you?

> After talking with many people, I have learned that we all have our own definition of black, white, and gray. Black and white for me is that I am either right or wrong. Good or bad. Judgement and condemnations. The gray area for me is living in the peace of God, and my ultimate goal is to reach a status of living in pure light, which I shall reach at the appointed time I am raised up to Heaven. I believe I will have great moments of living in the light, but to stay in constant light is impossible with my sinful nature and living in this sinful world. Yet living in the light is a daily choice to have hope, trust, and faith in God and His ways. Living in the dark means I am living with doubt and fear without hope. I will have moments in my life and in my future when I struggle with the dark, but it does not mean I am right or wrong, good or bad. It is an acceptance and acknowledgement that this is how the world works and the matter of most importance is my continued faith and hope in the Lord. Never give up!

16) What does protect your heart mean to you?

> Protecting my heart means I am to hold onto my beliefs and values as God shows them to me by studying His word. To protect and value these beliefs in my heart by not letting others come in and tell me what I should and should not believe or should and should not do. To stand up when I am confronted with love and respect of persons, but to exit those relationships with people who do not respect my stand or try to persuade me otherwise.

17) Are you living your beliefs, in action, in conversation, in relationships, in work, in talents, and in gifts?

> No, I am struggling with my beliefs. I believe I have some core beliefs that are to be Biblical in nature, yet are somehow twisted in the meaning to get me to conform to others wishes and not God's. I struggle with standing up for those beliefs because I get exhausted with fighting all the time. I strive to work on my relationships in a healthier way while standing up to my beliefs with confidence. I am aware this is not an overnight fix, but a day by day, step by step process. My talents and gifts are singing, which I struggle to do because it causes me a lot of pain, which is a trigger, but I am determined to continue with it as much as possible. My other talents are crafting and design. I have begun my own very small business to put my talents out there in hopes to build relationships and edify and love others to show them there is hope after much hurt.

Planting seeds! Beliefs come with sacrifices. What sacrifices are required for you to carry out your beliefs? In actions, in conversation, in relationships, in work, in talents, and in gifts? I must sacrifice those relationships that do not allow me or are constantly questioning my beliefs and values. No one has the right or authority to tell me what to believe and how I should act. Other sacrifices are to avoid certain subjects of sensitivity and share only with those who are supportive. Sacrifices of slowing down and doing short increments of work to help lessen my pain. To take time to relax, mindfulness, and meditation exercise. To exercise regularly and eat healthy. Use CBT skills when my mind is racing too much and to take medication when necessary. To balance my activities to not feel pressured and overwhelmed. To try to see myself as God does and not as I think others do. That my limitations are not weakness, but an opportunity for growth in patience and hope.

18) What are your weaknesses?

Caring what others think more highly than anything else. I have a driving force within me that seeks others approval. I am a people pleaser and a peace maker. My happiness comes when others are happy. It's like a codependency for me and I have to work very hard to not get caught up in it. Most of the time I am already caught up in pleasing others and I don't catch myself until I am so overwhelmed with burdens of doing for others.

I also struggle with misuse of core beliefs. One of the biggest core beliefs is the statement "But that is not Christlike" and what it really means. I second guess any decision that causes me to hold back or put up boundaries for my own sake. It's like a deep sense of putting others before yourself, yet when it comes down to it, I have nothing left of me to take care of myself. Before I know it everyone is asking, "what's wrong with you? Why are you acting so different?" Because I have to take a step back and make time to care for myself and let their needs go for a while. Another weakness I have is the guilt of being honest. I feel so much guilt and shame in being honest with my weaknesses. An overwhelming sense of I should not be like this, this is wrong so I should not put this down on paper as truth. I struggle with the should and should nots of this world and being accepting of the person I truly am. I am weak as accepting myself for who I am and being okay with it.

19) What are your strengths?

Determination is a big one. I am determined to get through this. If God brought me to it, then He will bring me through it. Not on my own but with his help and I am determined to try anything possible to get through. All these steps in this book I have done. There is nothing that I won't do when I am determined to persevere, and that is my next strength is perseverance. I have been through sexual abuse, emotional abuse, bullying, teenage pregnancy, illness, and more illness, mental breakdown, relationship issues, work issues. I am one walking basket case, but I will persevere. Honesty is my last one. I am honest to a fault. My honesty hurts others, puts me into the line of fire in stressful situations, but when all is said and done, I will be honest. Honest with how I feel, honest with how I see things, honest with my beliefs. It may cause me extra stress and trauma, but at the end of the situation I will have no regrets and I will always know who my support system is.

20) What are your likes and dislikes?

I like warm clear weather, but hate the cold.

I like the fall, but hate winter.

I like ice cream, but not fish.

I like music, but hate screaming.

I like time to myself, but hate when I get repeatedly interrupted.

I like sleep and hate it when I wake up throughout the night.

I like to look nice, but hate dressing up when I feel bad.

I like to socialize, but hate saying good-bye.

I like to work outside, but hate the feeling of being dirty.

I like to work with my hands, but hate to cook.

I like to write, but hate that I have to do it in small increments because sitting in a chair very long makes me hurt.

I like to paint, but hate cleaning the brushes.

I like to redecorate and make something new, but hate long projects.

I like to be taken seriously, but hate when people joke at my expense

I like to be in control, and hate spontaneity

I like to have healthy relationships, yet I am scared to put myself out there and get rejected.

I like to watch TV shows, but hate sitting still.

I like to read, but hate that it keeps me awake at night.

I like to crochet, but hate that it makes me hurt.

I like to learn new things, but hate the extreme concentration it takes to get it done.

I like my house to be clean, as well as my flower beds, and hate it when others notice when it's a mess

I like everything in its own place; I hate clutter.

I like being trusted and hate being second guessed.

21) What are your pet peeves?

Expectation to read other's minds
Being interrupted when I am trying to concentrate
Dirty feet on a clean floor
Constantly questioned and doubted
Being Viewed as weak just because I am small and quiet

22) What are your triggers?

Pain, suffering, time constrained pressures, certain people, confrontation, at times large crowds, being questioned, being dismissed without thought or care, not being believed.

23) What other questions can you think of that you need answers to, to find peace?

How does God see me? It is okay to love my self or put myself in front of others for my mental health? Next book loving yourself and biblical truths

Sources

https://www.biblegateway.com/blog/2012/06/what-was-the-original-language-of-the-bible/

The Holy Bible, King James Version. Cambridge Edition: 1769; King James Bible Online, 2020. www.kingjamesbibleonline.org.

http://www.history.com/news/7-historical-figures-posthumously-diagnosed-with-illnesses

https://chopra.com/articles/daily-practices-for-spiritual-mental-emotional-and-physical-well-being#sm.00001nytincdmlemiqv58uo1htpoa

https://wellness.ucr.edu/seven_dimensions.html

http://www.mkprojects.com/emotional-mental-spiritual-health

http://www.mkprojects.com/checklists-for-health

https://psychcentral.com/lib/15-common-cognitive-distortions/

https://psychcentral.com/lib/an-overview-of-dialectical-behavior-therapy/

https://en.wikipedia.org/wiki/Yoke